"This book skillfully and eloquently describes how our deepest longing for love is in fact the key to healing our personal wounds and the woundedness of the world at large. John Welwood's message echoes the Buddha's, showing us how we have direct access to the love and happiness we most long for, as our very essence."
—Sharon Salzberg, author of *Lovingkindness: The Revolutionary Art of Happiness*

"Full of practical wisdom and divinely inspired insight. A marvelous guide for any seeker choosing to walk on love's path."
—bell hooks, author of *All About Love: New Visions*

"Welwood's approach is noteworthy for its emphasis on learning how to receive love as well as give it. *Perfect Love, Imperfect Relationships* offers both grand theories and useful practices for incorporating these lessons into your life."
—*Body & Soul*

"With clear instructions and an even tone, Welwood shows us how to heal our psychic scars by opening up to the 'real love' available to us all at the core of our nature."—*Tricycle*

"Welwood challenges us to move from self-hatred to self-love and to do the inner work to embrace the love that sets us free."—*Spirituality & Health*

BOOKS BY JOHN WELWOOD

Perfect Love, Imperfect Relationships: Healing the Wound of the Heart (2005)

Toward a Psychology of Awakening: Buddhism, Psychotherapy, and the Path of Personal and Spiritual Transformation (2000)

Ordinary Magic: Everyday Life as Spiritual Path (1992)

Journey of the Heart: Intimate Relationship and the Path of Love (1990)

Challenge of the Heart: Love, Sex, and Intimacy in Changing Times (1985)

Awakening the Heart: East/West Approaches to Psychotherapy and the Healing Relationship (1983)

The Meeting of the Ways: Explorations in East/West Psychology (1979)

AUDIO BY JOHN WELWOOD

Perfect Love, Imperfect Relationships: A Workshop on Healing the Wound of the Heart (2007)

Perfect Love,
Imperfect Relationships

HEALING THE WOUND
OF THE HEART

JOHN WELWOOD

TRUMPETER
Boston & London
2007

Trumpeter Books
an imprint of Shambhala Publications, Inc.
Horticultural Hall
300 Massachusetts Avenue
Boston, Massachusetts 02115
www.shambhala.com

9 8 7 6 5

Printed in the United States of America

∞ This edition is printed on acid-free paper that meets
the American National Standards Institute z39.48 Standard.
♻ This book was printed on 30% postconsumer recycled paper.
For more information please visit www.shambhala.com.
Distributed in the United States by Random House, Inc.,
and in Canada by Random House of Canada Ltd

Library of Congress catalogues the previous edition of this book as follows:
Welwood, John, 1943–
Perfect love, imperfect relationships: healing the wound
of the heart / John Welwood.
    p. cm.
Includes bibliographical references.
ISBN 978-1-59030-262-0 (hardcover: alk. paper)
ISBN 978-1-59030-386-3 (paperback)
1. Love. 2. Interpersonal relations. I. Title.
BF575.L8W45 2005   158.2—dc22
2005009288

This book is dedicated to peace in the world.
May all beings know that they are loved—
so they may live at peace with themselves and all others.

Jump to your feet, wave your fists,
Threaten and warn the whole universe
That your heart can no longer live
Without real love!

—HAFIZ

Contents

Perfect Love, Imperfect Relationships

Introduction

A night full of talking that hurts,
My worst held-back secrets:
Everything has to do with loving and
not loving.

—RUMI

THE WORDS "I LOVE YOU," spoken in
moments of genuine appreciation, wonder, or caring, arise
from something perfectly pure within us—the capacity to
open ourselves and say yes without reserve. Such moments of
pure openheartedness bring us as close to natural perfection
as we can come in this life. The warm and radiant yes of the
heart is perfect, like the sun, in bringing all things to life and
nourishing all that is truly human.

Yet oddly enough, even though we may have glimpses of a
pure, bright love dwelling within the human heart, it's hard to
find it fully embodied in the world around us, especially
where it matters most—in our relationships with other people. Indeed, for many people today, risking themselves in a
love relationship has become a frightening proposition, a

near-certain prescription for overwhelming pain or emotional devastation. Scratch the surface of our sex-and-romance-crazed culture and you find a sense of disillusionment in many people where they feel, as one pop song puts it, that "love stinks." Or, as a young woman in one of my workshops expressed it: "If love is so great, why are relationships so impossible? Don't tell me I need to open my heart any more. My heart is already too open, and I don't want to keep getting hurt."

So right alongside the truth of love's perfection, there stands another, more difficult truth—the flawed, tangled web of human relationship, which gives rise to tremendous frustration, sorrow, and anger everywhere we look. One minute you're in touch with the love in your heart—you feel open, caring, and connected. And then the next minute, before you know it, you and your loved one have become embroiled in a conflict or misunderstanding that leads to shutting down or behaving in a heartless way.

Thus even when our love is genuine and real, something often seems to block its full and perfect expression in relationships. "I love you, but I can't live with you" is the classic statement of this painful gap between the pure love in our heart and the difficult relationships we inhabit. This disparity presents a maddening riddle, which each of us must "solve or be torn to bits," as D. H. Lawrence suggested.

This riddle shows up in many different guises. Even though love forever arises anew, most of us walk around feeling deprived of it, as if starving in a land of plenty. And while love can bring tremendous joy, our love life often brings our greatest suffering. Even though there is nothing as simple and straightforward as the warmth of the heart, still, "for one human being to love another, this is the most difficult of all our tasks," as the poet Rilke wrote. And while in one sense love conquers all, war nonetheless remains the governing force in world affairs.

The sense of loneliness and deprivation afflicting many people's lives is not because love is in short supply. For you can find love everywhere you look, in one form or another. Every smile and most of the conversations and glances you exchange with the people you encounter every day contain at least a few grains of love, in the form of interest, appreciation, consideration, warmth, or kindness. Add up all the interchanges you have with others every day and you will see that your life is sustained by a flow of interconnectedness, which is the play of love at work. "There is no force in the world but love," as Rilke writes.

Yet if love is the greatest power on earth, the force that sustains human life—which in some sense it certainly is—why hasn't love's radiant warmth been able to banish the darkness engulfing the world, and transform and uplift this earth? Why is it so hard for love to permeate the dense fabric of human relationships? If love is our greatest source of happiness and joy, why is it so hard to open to it fully and let it govern our lives? What is the problem?

These questions took on particular urgency for me soon after September 11, 2001, when the world was once again plunging into war. As the bombs rained down on Afghanistan in retaliation for the terrorist attacks in New York and Washington, the world felt especially fragile to me, and perilously close to collapsing into hatred and violence. After America's political leaders embarked on what appeared to be a war without end, I felt an imperative to take a fresh look at why it's so hard for what is best in the human being—the warmth and goodness of the heart—to take hold in this world.

I have previously written two books on conscious relationship—*Journey of the Heart* and *Love and Awakening*—that show how to embrace and work with the challenges of relationship as opportunities for personal transformation and spiritual awakening. This book takes a different tack. It focuses on the root source of all relational problems, "the mother of all relationship issues"—our wounded relationship to love itself.

The Mood of Unlove

There are hundreds of books on the market that offer relationship fixes in one form or another. Some of these techniques can be quite helpful. Yet at some point, most technical fixes turn out to be patches that fall off, for they fail to address what lies at the root of all interpersonal conflict and misunderstanding—whether between marital partners, family members, friends, fellow workers, or different ethnic groups in the world at large. All the most intractable problems in human relationships can be traced back to what I call *the mood of unlove*— a deep-seated suspicion most of us harbor within ourselves that we cannot be loved, or that we are not truly lovable, *just for who we are*. This basic insecurity makes it hard to trust in ourselves, in other people, or in life itself.

Not knowing, in our blood and bones, that we are truly loved or lovable undermines our capacity to give and receive love freely. This is the core wound that generates interpersonal conflict and a whole range of familiar relationship tangles. Difficulty trusting, fear of being misused or rejected, harboring jealousy and vindictiveness, defensively stonewalling, having to argue and prove we're right, feeling easily hurt or offended and blaming others for our pain—these are just a few of the ways that our insecurity about being loved or lovable shows up.

The mood of unlove often shows up in the form of sudden emotional flare-ups in reaction to any hint of being slighted or badly treated. It's as though a reservoir of distrust and resentment were ready and waiting to be released, which the tiniest incident can trigger. Even caring and compassionate people often carry within them a fair share of unlove and righteous grievance, which can suddenly erupt under certain circumstances. For some couples these explosions happen early on, blowing a budding relationship apart in their first few encounters. For others, the mood of unlove might not wreak its havoc until well into a seemingly happy marriage, when one or both partners suddenly wake up one day and realize they don't feel truly seen or known. It's not uncommon for long-term spouses to say something like, "I know my husband loves me, but somehow I don't *feel* loved."

Sometimes the mood of unlove shows up in the form of endless bickering and petty irritation, as though both partners were continually looking for reasons to grumble, "Why don't you love me better?" For example, one couple I worked with described the following incident that led to a weeklong estrangement. The woman had just made her husband tea when he became upset with her for putting milk in it: "Haven't I told you before that I don't want you putting milk in my tea for me, that I like to let it steep for a long time first?" The only way to understand how something so trivial could trigger a major conflict is through recognizing what her action signifies for him: In his eyes, she has shown once again that she is not attuned to him and his needs—like all the other women in his life, starting with his mother. And for her, when even making him tea becomes an occasion for blame and resentment, this shows, once again, that no matter what she does, she can never win his love. Lurking in the background of this petty incident is the age-old pain of feeling uncared for and unappreciated, which both partners are reenacting *once again*.

As a practicing psychotherapist, I have been intrigued by the tenacity and intransigence of the mood of unlove, which can live on in the psyche in spite of plenty of evidence to the contrary (even when people in our lives *do* love us) or in spite of many years of psychotherapy or spiritual practice. What's worse, the mood of unlove has the power to repel, belittle, or sabotage whatever love *is* there. Somehow the love that's available always seems to fall short—it's not sufficient, not good enough, or not the right kind. Somehow it fails to convince us that we are truly loved or lovable. In this way the mood of unlove—as an expectation that we won't or can't be fully embraced or accepted—makes us impervious to letting in the love that might actually free us from its grip.

As a result, "You have two choices in life: You can stay single and be misrable or get married and wish you were dead," as H. L. Mencken wrote with a flourish of wry, black humor. Reciting this line at relationship workshops always evokes peals of laughter as people feel the relief of naming this basic human dilemma. When under the spell of the mood of unlove, living alone is miserable because we feel bereft or abandoned. And yet marrying is no cure for this misery, since living with someone every day can further intensify the sense of unlove and make it feel even more hellish.

How then can brokenhearted people like ourselves heal this woundedness around love that has been passed down through the generations, and set ourselves free from the strife that dominates our world? This is the most crucial issue of human life, both personally and collectively. It is also the central focus of this book.

The Nature and Significance of Love

I would define love very simply: as a potent blend of openness and warmth, which allows us to make real contact, to take delight in and appreciate, and to be at one with—ourselves, others, and life itself. Openness—the heart's pure, unconditional yes—is love's *essence*. And warmth is love's basic *expression*, arising as a natural extension of this yes—the desire to reach out and touch, connect with, and nourish what we love. If love's openness is like the clear, cloudless sky, its warmth is like the sunlight streaming through that sky, emitting a rainbowlike spectrum of colors: passion, joy, contact, communion, kindness, caring, understanding, service, dedication, and devotion, to name just a few.

According to the saints and mystics, love is the very fabric of what we are; we are fashioned out of its warmth and openness. We don't have to be great sages to recognize this. All we need to do is take an honest look at what makes our life worthwhile. When the presence of love is alive and moving in us, there is no doubt that our life is on target and meaningful, regardless of our outer circumstances. We feel that we're *in touch,* connected with something larger than our small self. This lifts the burden of isolation and alienation off our shoulders, filling us with peace and well-being. But when the presence of love is absent, something often feels sad, not quite right; something seems to be missing, and it's hard to find much joy, even in the midst of favorable circumstances. We easily fall prey to meaninglessness, anxiety, or despair.

These simple truths are also upheld by neuroscience

research, which confirms that our connections with others affect the healthy development and functioning of the brain, the endocrine and immune systems, and our emotional balance. In short, love is the central force that holds our whole life together and allows it to function. In the words of the Indian sage Nisargadatta Maharaj, "Life is love and love is life."

While women generally recognize the central place of love in everything, men are more often more reluctant to acknowledge this. "Please don't reduce everything to that," I can hear many male readers groaning. "I have more important business to attend to than feeling loved." But think about it: The author who writes a best-seller, the politician who wins an election, the businessman who gains a promotion or an important contract—all feel good about themselves because a little love has flowed their way, in the form of recognition, praise, or appreciation. Even the trader who reaps a stock market windfall feels that the gods are smiling on him.

At bottom, most of the things we strive for—security, success, wealth, status, power, recognition, validation, praise—are ways of trying to fill a gaping hole within us, a hole formed out of our separation from love. As ways of trying to win love indirectly, these substitute gratifications do not truly nourish us, because they do not deliver the real thing. In that sense, they are like junk food. Their failure to truly nourish only intensifies our inner hunger, driving us to run all the harder on the hamster wheel of success, desperately hoping to win some reward that will truly satisfy.

Yet if love is so central to who we are, why do we often feel so separated from it? All the great spiritual traditions have addressed the question of why people treat each other so badly and the world is such a mess. They have provided various explanations for this, such as ignorance, bad karma, original sin, egocentricity, or the failure to recognize love as our very nature. Yet what is the root cause of these afflictions?

The Wound of the Heart

If we take an honest look within, we may notice a certain guardedness around our heart. For some people, this is a thick, impenetrable barricade. For others, it is a thinner, subtler protective shield or contraction that only emerges under threatening conditions. And nothing triggers this sense of threat so strongly as the suspicion discussed earlier: that we are not truly loved or acceptable as we are. Numbing or shutting down the heart is an attempt to deflect the pain of that.

Not knowing that we can be loved for who we are prevents us from trusting in love itself, and this in turn causes us to turn away from life and doubt its benevolence. We may tell ourselves that love is not really available. But the deeper truth is that we don't entirely trust it, and therefore have a hard time fully opening to it or letting it all the way into us. This disconnects us from our own heart, exacerbating our sense of love's scarcity.

This disconnection from love most often grows out of not feeling fully embraced or accepted in our family of origin—whether through neglect, lack of attunement, or outright abuse. Not feeling securely held in the arms of love, we fall into the grip of fear. Inadequate love and nurturance directly impact the child's sensitive nervous system, resulting in a certain degree of shock or trauma that will affect us for the rest of our life.

Sometimes the wounding or separation from love happens in more subtle ways. Some parents seem loving enough, yet they covertly or unconsciously dispense their love in controlling or manipulative ways. Or they may not be attuned to the child as someone different from them, a separate being in his or her own right. Such children may feel loved for certain attributes—but not for who they really are. In their need to please their parents and fit in, they come to regard love as something outside themselves, which they have to earn by living up to certain standards.

Children naturally try to protect themselves from the pain of inadequate love as best they can. They learn to separate and distance themselves from what causes them pain by contracting or shutting down. The technical term for this is *dissociation*.

Dissociation is our mind's way of saying no to and turning away from our pain, our sensitivity, our need for love, our grief and anger about not getting enough of it, and from our body as well, where these feelings reside. This is one of the most basic and effective of all the defensive strategies in the child's repertoire. Yet it also has a major downside: It constricts or shuts off access to two main areas of our body: the vital center in the belly—the source of desire energy, eros, vital power, and instinctual knowing—and the heart center—where we respond to love and feel things most deeply. In saying no to the pain of unlove, we block the pathways through which love flows in the body and thus deprive ourselves of the very nutrient that would allow our whole life to flourish. And so we wind up severing our connection to life itself.

This leaves us in a strange and painful dilemma. On one hand we hunger for love—we cannot help that. Yet at the same time, we also deflect it and refuse to fully open to it because we don't trust in it.

This whole pattern—not knowing we're loved as we are, then numbing our heart to ward off this pain, thereby shutting down the pathways through which love can flow into and through us—is the *wound of the heart*. Although this love-wound grows out of childhood conditioning, it becomes in time a much larger spiritual problem—a disconnection from the loving openness that is our very nature.

This universal human wound shows up in the body as emptiness, anxiety, trauma, or depression, and in relationships as the mood of unlove, with its attendant insecurity, guardedness, mistrust, and resentment. And all relationship problems follow from there.

Love and the wound of the heart always seem to go hand in hand, like light and shadow. No matter how powerfully we fall in love with someone, we rarely soar above our fear and distrust for very long. Indeed, the more brightly another person lights us up, the more this activates the shadow of our wounding and brings it to the fore. As soon as conflict, misunderstanding, and disappointment arise, a certain insecurity wells up from the dark recesses of the mind, whispering, "See, you're not really loved after all."

On the collective level, this deep wound in the human psyche leads to a world wracked by struggle, stress, and dissension. Communities and social institutions at every level—marriages, families, schools, churches, corporations, and nations all across the globe—are in disarray, divided against themselves. The greatest ills on the planet—war, poverty, economic injustice, ecological degradation—all stem from our inability to trust one another, honor differences, engage in respectful dialogue, and reach mutual understanding.

Thus all the beauty and the horrors of this world arise from the same root: the presence or absence of love. Not feeling loved and then taking that to heart is the only wound there is. It cripples us, causing us to shrivel and contract. Thus, apart from a few biochemical imbalances and neurological disorders, the diagnostic manual for psychological afflictions known as the DSM might as well begin: "Herein are described all the wretched ways people feel and behave when they do not know that they are loved." All hatred of ourselves and others; all our fear, egoism, communication problems, and sexual insecurities; all the pathology, neurosis, and destructiveness in the world; and the whole nightmare of history, with all its bloodshed and cruelty, boil down to one simple fact: Not knowing we are loved and lovable makes the heart grow cold. And all the tragedy of human life follows from there.

When people do not know they are loved, a cold black hole forms in the psyche, where they start to harbor beliefs that they're insignificant, unimportant, or lacking in beauty and goodness. This icy place of fear is what gives rise to terrorist attacks of all kinds—not just in the form of bombs going off, but also in the emotional assaults that go on within ourselves and our relationships.

Outer terror is but a symptom of inner terror. When people feel unloved or mistreated, they look for someone to blame, someone on whom they can take out their bad feelings. Though war and terrorism are usually regarded as political issues, the fact is that people in whom love is flowing freely do not throw bombs. Terrorism, like war itself, is a symptom of the disconnect from love that infects our world.

Unless we can eradicate this plague by healing the mood of unlove that has been passed down through the generations, the rule of fear and terror will never be overcome on this earth. A "war on terrorism" is an oxymoron, an impossibility, because you cannot eliminate terror through war, which only creates more terror. Only in an environment of love can we ever feel truly secure from attack. "We must love one another or die," as W. H. Auden wrote in a poem at the outbreak of World War II.

I recognize that some readers may regard it as naïve and unrealistic to introduce truths about love into discussions of political issues such as war and terrorism. Of course, wars, ethnic conflicts, and social injustice require political solutions. At the same time, political settlements that lack genuine caring and respect for all parties eventually fall apart and lead to new conflicts.

Leading religious and social activists have often understood the proclivity to war as a symptom of alienation from love, and emphasized the central role that love must play in solving the problems of the world. For example, Martin Luther King Jr. recognized the role that grievance plays in generating wars, arguing that only love can cure this illness: "Sooner or later all the people of the world will have to discover a way to live together in peace. . . . If this is to be achieved, man must evolve for all human conflict a method which rejects revenge, aggression and retaliation. The foundation of such a method is love."

This is a noble sentiment, yet how can humanity actually overcome its addiction to violence and its cynicism about love? What I suggest in this book is that war arises from grievance against others, and that this grievance is rooted in our love-wound—which we blame on others, taking it out on them. This book lays out a practical path for deeply understanding and addressing this core human problem.

Love and Grievance

My initial response to the terrorist attacks of 2001 and the war fever they unleashed was anger and indignation. Yet I soon saw that my reaction was part of the same problem that troubled me in the world at large. The terrorists had their righteous grievance against America; the American government had its righteous grievance against the terrorists. And like these warring parties, I too had a righteous grievance—against a world addicted to war and vengeance, and against purveyors of hatred on all sides. Despite my fervent wish for a world at peace, as long as I regarded terrorists and warmongers as some kind of adversary to harbor a grievance against, I too was putting on the mantle of war. Seeing how my investment in grievance was the very same thing that drives all the hatred and violence in the world catapulted me into a process of soul-searching and inner discovery.

My desire to understand how love's gold turns into lead forced me to take a long, hard look at grievance. In studying my own investment in grievance and how it operated in my relationships, I saw that something in me found great satisfaction in setting up an *other*—someone or something over against myself—and then making this other wrong, while making myself the injured party standing in righteous judgment. There was something about harboring a grievance, I had to admit, that was really quite compelling.

Everywhere we look, we find people indulging in the mind-set of grievance. Our marriages and families, schools and workplaces, have all become battlegrounds where people spend large amounts of precious life energy at war with one another, blaming and getting even. Then there is "grievance politics," where political campaigns manipulate people's dissatisfaction and anger, targeting convenient scapegoats as a way to win votes. Meanwhile, on the world stage various religious and ethnic groups continually engage in recrimination and retaliation against one another.

This tendency to set up adversaries to contend with is also at work inside ourselves. Perhaps you do daily battle with your job, regarding it as a devouring monster that threatens to consume you. Or maybe you struggle with your to-do lists, the various pressures in your life, the traffic, the weather, the difficult feelings coursing through you, or even life itself. Most painful of all is the inner battle that rages within your mind and body when you make *yourself* wrong or bad—which generates tremendous emotional stress and self-hatred. Some people even become so pitted against themselves that they wind up killing the monster they imagine themselves to be.

Why this compulsion to create adversaries and nurse grievances, when it only winds up destroying us and those around us? As I sifted through the layers of my grievance against the world in the aftermath of the terrorist attacks, I recognized an old sense of not belonging to this world—which I could trace back to childhood. I had felt like an alien while growing up because the adults around me seemed more interested in fitting me into their own agendas than in finding out who I might be. As a result of having to push my mother away because she could not let me be me, I had separated myself from love and remained on guard against it throughout the early decades of my life.

Consequently, I had learned to develop my intellect, at least in part, as a way of dissociating from the pain of this disconnection from love. Yet much deeper than any need to write, to accomplish, or to make a mark in the world, there was an undeniable longing that was humbling when I faced it in its unvarnished simplicity: At the root of everything I did, I had to admit, what I most wanted was to love and be loved.

At the bottom of my grievance against a world gone mad, I discovered the vulnerable child who still didn't know that love was fully available or truly reliable. Even though I seemingly had plenty of love in my life and had explored and written about intimate relationship for many years, I nonetheless uncovered a dark, hidden corner in myself where I did not entirely trust love. And I saw that this was where grievance took root—in this place where I stood pitted against a world that didn't seem friendly. Here in myself I was face-to-face with the same resentment that poisons the whole world, breeding all the blame and recrimination that eventually lead to violence, divorce, vendettas, and war. Recognizing this link between the mood of unlove and the mood of grievance within myself gave me a deeper understanding of why love continually goes awry in human relationships.

Wanting to explore this further, I decided to bring the question of grievance to the students in a class I was teaching while the terrorist attacks were still fresh and the level of fear and outrage was running high. I began by asking them to focus on a stressful situation in their lives. Then I asked them to look at how their current stress was linked to setting themselves in opposition to something they treated as an adversary. Some people chose a relationship or work-related situation to focus on; others took the terrorist acts, our government's response, or the chaos in the world.

My students found it illuminating to see how, in each case, their tension grew out of saying no to something they were treating as an adversary. Next I asked them to see if they could find in this struggle some old, familiar grievance against others that went back all their life. And I asked them to state this grievance in one sentence, in the present tense, starting with "You . . ." Here are some of the grievance statements they came up with:

"You want to take advantage of me."

"You don't value me for who I am."

"You don't care about me; you're only interested in yourself."

"You want to control me."

"You don't see me."

"You don't respect me."

"You want to do me in."

"You don't accept me unless I fit into your agenda."

"You use me for your own ends."

"You don't give me your time and attention."

"You make me wrong for what I need."

"You don't recognize my goodness."

As people took turns stating their grievance, it became clear that these were all different forms of the same complaint, the most fundamental sorrow that there is: You don't love me. More specifically: *You don't love me as I am*. This is the universal wound that fuels our fight with the world.

Love is the recognition of beauty. Each of us longs to know and feel confident in the beauty and goodness that lies within us. Especially as children, we needed someone else to see the beauty of our soul and to reflect this beauty back to us, like a mirror, so we could see and appreciate it ourselves. When the beauty of who we are was not recognized, we felt the absence of love, and our system went into shock and shut down.

For reasons we could not fathom, other people, God, or life itself seemed to be depriving us of the recognition and understanding we instinctively knew we needed in order to thrive. This was maddening. We knew that love was rightfully ours and that we needed to be at one with it, to feel it filling and permeating us, through and through. Someone or something was surely to blame! So we formed a grievance against other people or life itself for not providing the love we needed, or against ourselves for not having succeeded at winning that love.

Great Love

It's true, we are entitled to perfect love. It's our birthright. But the problem is that we are looking for it in the wrong places—outside ourselves, in our imperfect relationships with imperfect people who are wounded like we are. This inevitably leaves us frustrated and disappointed. Even though perfect love can shine through relationships in moments, we cannot count on other people as a consistent source of it.

Yet even though human love usually manifests imperfectly, there is another dimension of love that *is* perfect, unbroken, and always available. It flows directly into the heart from the ultimate source of all—whether we call that God, Tao, or Buddha-nature. This is great love, absolute love—pure, unconditional openness and warmth—which actually abides at the very core of our nature.

If great love is like the sun, our woundedness is like a cloud cover temporarily blocking its rays. Fortunately, just as the sun cannot be damaged by clouds, so our native capacity for warmth and openness cannot be destroyed. Thus healing the wound of the heart does not require fixing something that is broken. Having a wounded heart is more like being lost—lost in the clouds that temporarily block access to the sun that is always shining. Though we can spend a whole lifetime lost in these clouds, this doesn't mean that the sun itself is lost or damaged. Healing the love-wound, then, involves making ourselves available to the sun, that it may do what it naturally wants to do: shine upon us.

Letting Love In

Most religions try to remedy the problem of human love-lessness by admonishing us to love more generously. The way to be loved, they say, is first to love. "To him who hath shall be given." " 'Tis better to give than to receive."

This core principle of spiritual life certainly contains profound truth. Yet there is another truth that stands alongside it: We cannot give what we cannot receive. Just as the earth is abundant because of its ability to receive and absorb (light from the sun and rain from the sky), so we can only give forth love abundantly if we are able to receive it, soak it up, and be nourished by it. If we don't feel loved within ourselves, then how can we ever truly love? If our wounding prevents us from letting love in, then how much do we have to give?

"To love is to cast light," Rilke writes, while "to be loved means to be ablaze." Who is to say that being ablaze is any less holy than casting light? And how can we cast pure light if we are not ablaze?

Thus the key to loving is to become more permeable to love, to let it all the way into us, so that it can live and breathe from inside out. Even if we believe that God is love or that we have a moral duty to love our neighbor, such beliefs will have little effect as long as our "in-channel" is shut down or constricted, preventing great love from flowing freely into and through us.

Countless books have been written about how to do a better job of loving. This book is different because it will help you focus instead on your capacity to receive love and how you can go about opening up that capacity.

There is a secret about human love that is commonly overlooked: Receiving it is much more scary and threatening than giving it. How many times in your life have you been unable to let in someone's love or even pushed it away? Much as we proclaim the wish to be truly loved, we are often afraid of that, and so find it difficult to open to love or let it all the way in.

One way that couples often deal with their fear of receiving love is to split into two poles—one partner becoming the pursuer and the other the distancer. Although it looks as though the distancer is the one who is afraid of letting love in, in fact both sides are choosing control over receptivity. Pursuers remain in control by demanding, seducing, or chasing after—all of which keep them from having to melt and open. They are often frightened of having to receive and respond—which is why they would rather do the chasing. Distancers remain in control by withholding. While each side complains about the other, they are in fact doing the same thing: engaging in a strategy that avoids the risk of opening fully to love.

A Psychospiritual Approach

In my work as a psychotherapist, I have discovered the power of bringing together both psychological and spiritual principles in the process of healing and growth. Psychological work focuses more on what has gone wrong: how we have been wounded in our relations with others and how to go about addressing that. Spiritual work focuses more on what is intrinsically right: how we have infinite resources at the core of our nature that we can cultivate in order to live more expansively. If psychological work thins the clouds, spiritual work invokes the sun. This book brings these two approaches together, presenting a *psychospiritual* approach to transforming the wound of the heart.

On the psychological level, this book offers a distinctive set of understandings and concrete methods for addressing your personal wounding around love and releasing your old grievances so that you can let love flow more freely in and through you. On the spiritual level, it will help you develop your capacity to open, to hold your most difficult experiences in a space of love, and beyond that, to tap into the great force of absolute love that is your very essence, so that it may infuse and illumine your life from within.

Working on both these levels—addressing your psychological wounding and learning to access great love—will help you relate to yourself, others, and all of life with a more generous, open heart. You will discover that your wounding is not a fault or defect but rather a guiding compass that can lead to greater connectedness. And this will allow you to live more creatively with the tension between love's inherent perfection and relationship's inevitable imperfection.

All the ideas and methods in this book have grown out of my own personal experience and research, as well as my work as a psychotherapist. In sharing this material with people in my classes and workshops, I have seen it have a powerful effect on their relations with themselves and others. In a teaching context, experiential exercises provide a way to apply this material to their lives in a concrete, personal way and make it their own. Yet since including exercises in the body of a book can interfere with the flow of the prose, I have chosen to gather some of these exercises, with a few important exceptions, in a separate section at the back of the book, organized by chapter. If you are so inclined, you can turn to this section and work with the exercises after reading each chapter. This will aid you in integrating and incorporating the understandings that you gain along the way.

May all beings be happy and at their ease. Through knowing we are held in love, may we find the boundless source of joy within ourselves and share this with the world around us. May we realize our true nature as blissful, radiant love.

Prologue
To Feel Held in Love

David was an interesting mix: He was an engaging male in his forties who had deep feeling for women, for sex, and for honest, direct contact. Yet he also lived under the shadow of his wound, and his life was marked by a series of love affairs that had never gone very far. While he had no trouble finding attractive female partners, the story was always the same: He would wind up either judging them and pushing them away or holding back until they finally left. He desperately wanted love in his life, and as he looked back on all the women he had split up with, he admitted that several of them could have made good mates. Yet at the time, he had always found something to justify his dissatisfaction and subsequent exit. He had entered therapy because he wanted to find out what was wrong with his love life.

Six months earlier he had embarked on a new relationship with a woman whom he loved more wildly and intensely than anyone before. They shared a strong emotional bond, great talks, and terrific sex. But at a certain point, he pulled back and cut off the relationship with Lynn because he couldn't trust her and feared how much she could hurt him.

In our first few sessions, David remained focused on Lynn and her untrustworthiness, but I eventually steered the focus back to what was going on within him. He had grown up with a mother who was erratic, depressed, and largely unavailable for long periods of time, and when she was there, she had little to give emotionally. Nothing David did—from getting angry to withdrawing—brought him the attention and love he needed. As a result, he simply didn't trust that love could really be there for him or that he could be loved for who he was. He would wind up trying to prove his worth by impressing women, all the while resenting them for having to do this.

Underneath David's engaging exterior was a seething resentment he could barely recognize, much less express, because in his family anger had been the ultimate sin that warranted rejection. So one way he expressed his anger was to push away anyone who tried to get close. He was essentially saying to all the women who wanted him, "Get lost, I don't trust your interest and attraction because you could never really love me." The distrust he felt toward Lynn reverberated down the corridors of his whole past, a whole lifetime of never feeling fully loved or embraced.

After a number of weeks of working with and understanding his wounding, David's interest in Lynn started to revive and he wanted to see her again, even though it felt dangerous. As he considered this, there was a wonderful moment when he looked up, as if gazing to heaven, and asked, almost rhetorically, "So is that it? You love someone and open yourself and feel vulnerable, you let them in and they become really important to you, and then they can just do anything they want—walk away, hurt you, lie to you—and there's nothing you can do about it? Is that what love's about?"

The rawness of David's words touched a chord that resonated in me, putting me in touch with my own experience of what he was speaking about, and I smiled in recognition. I reflected on how when you really want deep connection with someone, when that passion wells up from deep within, it's like a wave you can't control. It simply busts you open. Not only can't you control the wave of feeling, you also can't control how the other person will respond to you. I thought of times I'd felt raw like that, and the fear and instinct to protect myself that came along with it.

"When I feel this open to someone, I can really feel the depth and power of it," David went on to say. "I know this is what I really want with someone, and that's where the real juice lies." He was speaking of that sweet edge of surrender where the force of love carries us along, making us want to keep opening without putting on the brakes. "But it feels so dangerous, like I could get killed."

David was standing on a razor's edge, uncertain whether to give in to the pull of his attraction to Lynn—which felt terribly risky—or stand back and play it safe. I asked him, "If you could have whatever you want in this relationship, what would that be?" The first words out of his mouth were a plaintive, "I don't know." I encouraged him to sit longer with the question, look inside, and allow an answer to arise from deeper within. After a pause, he said, "I'd like to be able to trust her and know that I was really loved." Hardly had these words left his mouth than he qualified them: "But maybe that's too much to ask for." I asked, "What would it be like to feel loved like that? What would that give you?" A longer pause now, and then: "A sense of acceptance, of being valued for who I am."

My next question was: "And what would that give you—if you felt really accepted and valued?" An even longer pause this time, after which he said softly, "I'm so tired of being separate and alone. I really want to feel connected. . . . ." David had often talked about a recurring sense of isolation that left him feeling as though he were lost in this world and didn't belong anywhere. This was the first time he had directly acknowledged his longing to feel connected.

Yet I could sense that something more was stirring in him. I invited him to continue this inquiry, asking him what that sense of connection would give him. This time the answer came quickly, before he could think about it: "A feeling of belonging, like I was cherished just for who I was—though I'm not sure what that would be like, because, you know, I've never experienced that."

The color rose in David's face after these words, and I recognized the leap they represented for him. We talked about this for a while, acknowledging how hard it is for men to recognize their desire to belong and feel cherished, and how it is even rarer and more vulnerable to admit this to another man. David searched my face for signs of judgment, so I let him know I was right there with him, appreciating his willingness to share this with me. We sat for a while in silence, both sensing what it was like for him to acknowledge his longing to be loved like this.

Part of me wanted to stop there and leave well enough alone. Yet having come this far, I sensed that there was something more to explore here. After making sure he was still okay, I said, "Imagine being cherished, and see what that gives you on the inside, what it allows you to experience inside yourself." He closed his eyes for a while, then said, "It feels like being held, held in someone's loving arms. . . . I can actually feel that a little bit right now."

David and I were both noticeably softening here, together. The warmth, clarity, and groundedness that David was experiencing were filling the room.

Having felt so disconnected from his family as a child, David's willingness to acknowledge his need to belong, to feel cherished, and to be held in love represented important steps toward healing his alienation. In directly acknowledging these deep needs and allowing them to be there, David was holding his own experience in warmth and openness. And this gave him a taste of what it was like to feel held in love and acceptance—which was what he was looking for.

We had come a long way, and again I was tempted to leave it at that. Yet before I knew it, the next question sprang to my lips: "What's that like for you—to feel held like that? How does that affect you in your body?" The answer this time was right at hand because David was already there: "It feels like I've landed on the ground, which is holding me up. There's a warmth in my chest and a fullness in my belly."

"What happens when you stay present with the feelings in your belly and chest?"

"It's relaxing. Something in me lets down."

I encouraged him to let himself relax into this. Since this was a new and powerful experience for him, it was important to let his body get to know it more fully. After a while, he said, "There's a blissful sense of warmth spreading through my body, as if it's permeating all my cells." David was experiencing what it was like to let love move freely through him, and I encouraged him to keep letting himself have this full-body blissful experience. And then a final question: "What's that like—to let love move through you?"

"It's like coming in for a landing, and settling in. . . . It's like deep rest. . . . It feels like all of me is here."

"There's no need to prove yourself right now."

"No, nothing to prove. I can just be."

We had reached the bottom of the inquiry. He had landed in the only place there is to land—in his own nature, that presence of openness and warmth that we call love, goodness, or beauty. And he felt this in his body as a fullness in the belly and an openness in the heart. This was, at bottom, David's deepest wish: to go beyond having to prove himself in order to win love, to relax and settle into being himself, to reconnect with his vitality center and his heart. Recognizing this, he felt a deep sense of peace washing over him as he let himself rest there—present in himself, to himself, with himself.

This proved to be a major turning point in our work together. David had uncovered a clear, flowing spring in the middle of the desert of alienation where he had wandered all his life. And this allowed him to approach his relationship with Lynn in a new way, from a stronger place, more rooted in himself.

Love as a Holding Environment

The key moments in this session were David's recognition of his deep need to feel held in love and his discovery of what that holding felt like, which allowed him to relax, let down, and settle into himself. David's distrust of his mother had led him to fear and resent women all of his life. But at an even deeper level, his wound showed up as a distrust of life, a difficulty recognizing that his whole existence was held by something larger that he could trust.

What exactly is the nature of this holding that we need?

Consider for a moment how all things in this universe are held by something larger. The earth is held in space, which is the all-encompassing environment that allows it to move and turn freely. DNA is held within cells, and cells are held within the larger tissues and organs of the body. Leaves are held by a tree, trees are held by the earth. And growing children are held within a family environment.

The British child psychiatrist D. W. Winnicott defined the family as a "holding environment" that allows and supports the healthy growth of the child. Beyond the physical holding that is essential for children, Winnicott's notion refers to a benevolent emotional environment that a family can provide.

What type of holding is most essential for human development? Imagine picking up a baby bird that has fallen from its nest. If you hold it too tightly, you crush it. If you hold it too loosely, it falls to the ground. So you want to cradle it in your hands, but you also don't want to press too hard against it.

These, then, are the two essential aspects of holding: contact and space. Contact involves meeting, seeing, touching, attunement, connection, and care. When children experience good contact, they are more likely to develop confidence, inner support, and self-acceptance. But good contact by itself is not enough. Children also need to be given space—room to be, to be themselves. Contact without space can become intrusive, claustrophobic, smothering.

Winnicott stressed the importance of allowing infants to rest in their own "unstructured being," without constant intrusion. When parents fail to provide this spaciousness, children feel smothered or controlled. Then they become overly oriented toward pleasing the parents and fitting into the parents' designs, thus losing touch with their own sense of being.

When parents are nonintrusive, when they recognize and

honor their child's individual rhythms and needs, when they respect the child's space instead of continually interrupting the child's "going-on-being" (as Winnicott calls it), this helps the child rest at ease in himself or herself. Of course, if this spaciousness is not balanced by good contact, that too becomes problematic, for then the child feels abandoned.

Thus there are two general types of wounding around love that lead to fear of intimacy. When parents act intrusively and do not provide enough space, then children grow up fearing that close contact with others threatens them with engulfment, control, manipulation, or violation. And when parents do not provide warm emotional contact, then children grow up fearing that relationships will lead to abandonment, loss, or deprivation. Engulfment fears generally lead to withdrawal in relationships, while abandonment fears lead to clinging, though these two types of wounding can also show up in a variety of other symptoms. Many people suffer from some of each, resulting in "push-pull" relationships where one partner pursues when the other is pulling away, but then retreats when the other comes forward.

When parents do provide enough of both contact and space, this creates a holding environment that nurtures healthy development and healthy relationship. In this kind of friendly environment, children can feel safe to relax, let go, and trust. And this helps them to keep the heart channel open and to experience its delicate sensitivity, which the Tibetan meditation master Chögyam Trungpa called "the soft spot."

The two aspects of holding—contact and space, attunement and letting be—correspond to the two core qualities of love, warmth and openness, that are native to our being. Warmth is our natural impulse to reach outside ourselves, touch, and make contact, to welcome, embrace, and take delight in. Openness is our capacity to let be, to allow, to let in and receive others as they are, in a gentle, spacious way, without having to dominate them or bend them to our will. This kind of letting be is the greatest kindness we can offer those we love. Taken together, openness and warmth allow us to recognize and appreciate the natural beauty at the core of everything and everyone—in short, to love.

Even though these two qualities are part of our native birthright, they need an initial spark to ignite them. For children, that spark is knowing that they are loved. And children know they are loved when they feel genuinely held, that is, when their parents provide both warm contact and gentle space that lets them be.

To feel held in love, then, is the key, as it was for David, to letting down our guard, so that we can learn to relax, let love flow through us, and reside in the essential openness of our own heart.

CHAPTER ONE

Perfect Love, Imperfect Relationships

Again and again it defeats me—
This reliance on others for bliss.

—FROM A POEM BY THE AUTHOR

IF THE PURE ESSENCE OF LOVE is like the sun in a cloudless sky, this clear and luminous light shines through relationships most brightly in beginnings and endings. When your baby is first born, you feel so graced by the arrival of such an adorable being that you respond to it totally, without reserve, demand, or judgment. Or when you first fall in love, you are so surprised and delighted by the sheer beauty of this person's presence that it blows your heart wide open. For a while the bright sunlight of all-embracing love pours through full strength, and you may melt into bliss. Similarly, when a friend or loved one is dying, all your quibbles with that person fall away. You simply appreciate the other just for who he or she is, just for having been here with you in this world for a little while. Pure, unconditional love shines through when people put themselves—their own demands and agendas—aside and completely open to one another.

Absolute love is not something that we have to—or that we even can—concoct or fabricate. It is what comes through us naturally when we fully open up—to another person, to ourselves, or to life. In relation to another, it manifests as selfless caring. In relation to ourselves, it shows up as inner confidence and self-acceptance that warms us from within. And in relation to life, it manifests as a sense of well-being, appreciation, and joie de vivre.

Absolute Love

When we experience this kind of openness and warmth coming from another, it provides essential nourishment: It helps us experience our own warmth and openness, allowing us to recognize the beauty and goodness at the core of our nature. The light of unconditional love awakens the dormant seed potentials of the soul, helping them ripen, blossom, and bear fruit, allowing us to bring forth the unique gifts that are ours to offer in this life. Receiving pure love, caring, and recognition from another confers a great blessing: It affirms us in being who we are, allowing us to say yes to ourselves.

When two people see and appreciate each other as they are, they share a moment of I-Thou recognition, as Martin Buber would call it. Buber sees this as providing a certain kind of essential confirmation: It helps us know and feel *that we are.*

What feels most affirming is not just to feel loved but to

feel loved as we are. *As we are* means *in our very being.* Absolute love is the love of being.

Deeper than all our personality traits, pain, or confusion, our being is the dynamic open presence that we essentially are. It is what we experience when we feel settled, grounded, and connected with ourselves. When rooted in this basic ground of presence, love flows freely through us, and we can more readily open up to others. When two people meet in this quality of open presence, they share a perfect moment of absolute love.

However—and this is an essential point—the human personality is not the source of absolute love. Rather, its light shines through us, from what lies altogether beyond us, the ultimate source of all. We are the channels through which this radiance flows. Yet in flowing through us, it also finds a home within us, taking up residence as our heart-essence.

We have a natural affinity for this perfect food that is also our deepest essence, our life's blood. That is why every baby instinctively reaches out for it from the moment of birth. *We cannot help wanting our own nature.*

When the value and beauty of our existence is recognized, this allows us to relax, let down, and settle into ourselves. In relaxing, we open. And this opening makes us transparent to the life flowing through us, like a fresh breeze that enters a room as soon as the windows are raised. This brings a sense of well-being, as well as genuine power, which D. H. Lawrence defines as "life rushing into us."

Martin Buber sees the moment of I-Thou connection as the shedding of an old, protective sheath, like a butterfly's emergence from its chrysalis. In tasting pure, unconditional love, we experience that it's good to be ourselves, good to be alive, and this makes us want to spread our wings and soar. This influx of aliveness coursing through us feels blissful.

In this way, experiencing unconditional love allows us to *rest in ourselves and the blissful flow of our aliveness*. As Brother David Steindl-Rast describes this deep connectedness: "We simply know for a moment that all belongs to us because we belong to all."

This is one of the great gifts of human love, this entry it provides into something even greater than human relatedness. In helping us connect with the radiant aliveness within us, it reveals our essential beauty and power, where we are one with life itself because we are fully transparent to life. When life belongs to you and you belong to life, this sets you free from hunger and fear. You experience the essential dignity and nobility of your existence, which does not depend on anyone else's approval or validation. In this deep sense of union with life, you realize you are not wounded, have never been wounded, and cannot be wounded.

This is the bottom line of human existence: Absolute love helps us connect with who we really are. That is why it is indispensable.

Relative Love

Yet even though the human heart is a channel through which great love streams into this world, this heart channel is usually clogged with debris—fearful, defensive patterns that have developed out of not knowing we are truly loved. As a result, love's natural openness, which we can taste in brief, blissful moments of pure connection with another person, rarely permeates our relationships completely. Indeed, the more two people open to each other, the more this wide-openness also brings to the surface all the obstacles to it: their deepest, darkest wounds, their desperation and mistrust, and their rawest emotional trigger-points. Just as the sun's warmth causes clouds to arise by prompting the earth to release its moisture, so love's pure openness activates the thick clouds of our emotional wounding, the tight places where we are shut down, where we live in fear and resist love.

There is good reason why this happens: Before we can become a clear channel through which love can freely flow, the ways we are wounded must come to the surface and be exposed. Love as a healing power can operate only on what presents itself to be healed. As long as our wounding remains hidden, it can only fester.

This, then, is *relative love:* the sunlight of absolute love as it becomes filtered through the clouds of our conditioned personality and its defensive patterns—fearfulness, distrust, reactivity, dishonesty, aggression, and distorted perception. Like a partly cloudy sky, relative love is incomplete, inconstant, and imperfect. It is a continual play of light and shadow. The full radiance of absolute love can only sparkle through in fleeting moments.

If you observe yourself closely in relationships, you will see that you continually move back and forth between being open and closed, clear skies and dark clouds. When another person is responsive, listens well, or says something pleasing, something in you naturally starts to open. But when the other is not responsive, can't hear you, or says something threatening, you may quickly tense up and start to contract.

Our ability to feel a wholehearted yes toward another person fluctuates with the changing circumstances of each moment. It depends on how much each of us is capable of giving and receiving, the chemistry between us, our limitations and conditioned patterns, how far along we are in our personal development, how much awareness and flexibility we each have, how well we communicate, the situation we find our-selves in, and even how well we have each slept the night be-fore. *Relative* means *dependent on time and circumstance*.

Ordinary human love is always relative, never consistently absolute. Like the weather, relative love is in continual dy-namic flux. It is forever rising and subsiding, waxing and wan-ing, changing shape and intensity.

So far all of this may seem totally obvious. Yet here's the rub: We imagine that others—surely someone out there!—should be a source of perfect love by consistently loving us in just the right way. Since our first experiences of love usually happen in relation to other people, we naturally come to re-gard relationship as its main source. Then when relation-ships fail to deliver the ideal love we dream of, we imagine something has gone seriously wrong. And this disappointed hope keeps reactivating the wound of the heart and gener-ating grievance against others. This is why the first step in healing the wound and freeing ourselves from grievance is to appreciate the important difference between absolute and relative love.

At the deepest level of our being—the divinity within that we share with all beings—there is no separation between me and you. At any moment it is possible to experience the warmth and openness of a heart connection with any living creature: a lover, a child, a friend, a stranger passing on the street, or even a dog. When we appreciate the beauty of an-other's being, the heart channel opens and a spark of absolute love passes through us. In this moment of connection we no longer feel so separate or isolated. We delight in sharing the one lovely, tender presence that dwells in the heart of all.

Yet at the same time, on the relative plane, we always re-main separate and different. We inhabit separate bodies, with different histories, backgrounds, families, character traits, values, preferences, perspectives, and, in the end, different destinies. We each see and respond to things differently, and approach life in our own unique way.

Yes, we can experience moments of being at one with another. But this can happen only when we connect being-to-being, because at the level of pure being and pure openness, we *are* one. My openness is not different from your openness, because openness has no solid form and therefore no boundary that separates us, one from the other. Therefore, when we meet in a moment of absolute love, *being-to-being*, it is like water poured into water.

Relative love, by contrast, is an exchange that occurs on the level of form, *person-to-person*. Every person, just like every snowflake, every tree, every place, every circumstance in this world, is completely distinct. Each of us has our own unique character and way of unfolding, different from all others. While two persons can know themselves as one in the realm of pure openness, they remain irrevocably two in the realm of form.

One night you connect deeply with another, which leaves you feeling wide open to this person, totally amorous and enamored. But then the next morning, though you may still feel loving, that wide-openness may become clouded by considerations that start to arise: Is it safe to open yourself to this person? Can you accept the ways this person is totally different from you? How deeply is he or she able to understand you? Are you a good match?

Melting into oneness provides moments of blissful union in absolute love. And this is what the great mythic romances thrive on, this pure discovery and meeting that often happens outside ordinary time and space. But the challenges of relative love bring couples back to earth, forcing them to continually face and work with their twoness. This is not a bad thing, however. For without honoring the ways in which they are distinctly different, and exploring how to keep finding each other across these differences, a couple's connection will lose passion and vibrancy, and run the risk of unhealthy emotional fusion or codependency.

Thus relationships continually oscillate between two people finding common ground and then having that ground slip out from under them as their differences pull them in different directions. While trying to meet in the present moment, they become tossed around by shifting tides of memories, expectations, and wounds from the past. This ongoing tension between oneness and twoness, togetherness and separateness, fresh moments of discovery and old associations, inevitably renders relative love unsteady and unstable.

This is a problem only when we expect it to be otherwise, when we imagine that love should manifest as a steady state. That kind of expectation prevents us from appreciating the special gift that relative love does have to offer: personal intimacy. Intimacy—the sharing of who we are in our distinctness—can happen only when my partner and I meet as two, when I appreciate the ways she is wholly other, and yet not entirely other at the same time.

While the play of twoness and oneness generates sparks of curiosity and passion, it also ensures that intimacy can be only intermittent at best. Intimate moments, in which we make contact across the great divide of our differences, are just that—moments—rather than a constant, steady flow. At its best, relative love has a great beauty all its own, which sparkles through when two people can appreciate and enjoy each other in the midst of their differences and the changes they are going through. At its worst, however, it becomes the stuff of soap opera and tragedy.

So if you are counting on a steady state of attunement with another person, you are setting yourself up for frustration, disappointment, and anguish, because this is impossible. Each person can only follow his or her own internal laws. Since everyone has his or her own rhythm and sensibility, you can never count on others to be consistently attuned to you. It's inevitable to fall out of synch with your beloved, since you both invariably want different things—from each other and from life—at different times. As a result, harmony inevitably turns into dissonance, and understanding into misunderstanding, creating hurt and separation. Thus even the closest of marriage partners wind up at times feeling misunderstood, disconnected, or utterly alone.

Even someone who wanted to be perfectly attuned to us would be unable to, for he or she could never divine exactly what we want at each moment. Maybe we want closeness right now, so our lover snuggles up to us, but then a few moments later, we want some space. It is hard enough for us to know what we want and what's going on inside from moment to moment, and besides, it's always changing. If that is so, how can we expect anyone else to be consistently attuned to us, especially when others can only operate according to their own very different perceptions, rhythms, and needs?

Not only do we each have different needs and perspectives, we often want to be loved in a very particular way—one that would soothe our emotional wounding from the past. But that is a tall order, for it assumes that others should consistently tailor their style of loving to match our style. If you have abandonment fears, for example, you might press your partner for more verbal engagement than he or she is comfortable with. That kind of engagement might be soothing for you; it lets you know the other is there for you. Unfortunately, these expectations may trigger your partner's engulfment fears, for he or she may feel controlled when pressed for engagement on your timetable. Unlike you, your partner may feel most loved when given space to be himself or herself. So if you expect your partner to love you in just the right way, this may make him or her want to withdraw, which in turn will activate your abandonment fears. Despite their best efforts, two partners often cannot help triggering each other's wounds in this way.

Even though no one can provide consistent attunement, we may go on expecting it nonetheless, while blaming others for its absence: "You did not give me my due." As one Indian teacher, Swami Prajnanpad, describes this: "Everyone is passing through this deep mental agony. Why? Because he wants to have, but does not get. He believes that he ought to get and that it can be gotten. And yet he didn't get. This is what is causing such pangs of agony."

The question here is, are we ourselves acting with love when we try to get others to love us the way we think they should? Isn't this a form of control? Expectations in relationships can often be a subtle form of violence, for they can be a demand that others conform to our will.

In all of these ways, then, relative love makes for a bumpy ride. After an intimate moment of I-Thou communion, we inevitably return to seeing the one we love as "other," someone "over there" who becomes the object of our needs, reactions, or designs. "This is the exalted melancholy of our fate," writes Buber, "that every Thou in our world must become an It. . . . Genuine contemplation never lasts long . . . and love cannot persist [in a pure state]. Every Thou in the world is doomed to become a thing or enter into thinghood again and again." Even though pure love may be our heart essence, its expression is continually subject to past conditioning and present conditions. Though a mother may love her child unconditionally, if she suddenly becomes upset by something he just did, or if she is having a bad day, she may treat him unkindly.

We cannot avoid this fate, this fall into separateness, where we make ourselves and everything we love into an object of our hopes and fears. Thus relationships continually stray from the joy of I-Thou communion into the turbulence of like and dislike, agreement and disagreement, closeness and distance. Your husband might be kind and patient today, but tomorrow all of his hidden rage may come spilling out. One moment pure love sparkles through your beloved's eyes, while the next moment you say the wrong thing and she is glaring at you.

Pure love operates on the absolute plane, while like and dislike operate on a different level, on the relative, personal plane. Understanding that we live on both of these levels helps to relieve the confusion of feeling "I love you, but right now I can't stand you." We cannot help liking those aspects of other people that accord with our tastes and preferences while disliking things in them that rub us the wrong way. Only at an advanced level of spiritual development can human beings ever become free from the push and pull of like and dislike. This means that relative love inevitably contains a certain amount of ambivalence, or mixed feelings.

Thus husband and wife, parent and child, friend and friend, can never maintain a steady state of harmony or communion. It is in the nature of things that every movement of coming together is followed by moving apart. This is not a design flaw or fault—of love, of human beings, or of the universe. It doesn't mean you're bad or others are bad or life's unfair or anything like that. The pulse of life forever moves in cycles of up and down, back and forth, expansion and contraction, synergy and entropy.

Energy moves in waves, and waves by definition have peaks and troughs. You cannot have a peak unless it is preceded by a trough. Coming together can only happen when it is preceded by separation, and understanding when it is preceded by lack of understanding.

Indeed, if relationship did not rise and fall like this, it would become stagnation and bondage rather than a dynamic dance. Relative human love is imperfect and impermanent, just like everything else on this earth. And human experience is always raw, unfinished, messy. Nothing lasts. Nothing stays the same. There is no final fulfillment that maintains itself once and for all. Everything is subject to revision.

When the delightful high points of new love are followed by low points of conflict and suffering, however, we often regard this as a disaster that shouldn't be happening. But if we can recognize these lows as the unavoidable troughs of relative love's wave, then misunderstanding and separation can more readily become a springboard for new understanding and connection.

If we look honestly at our lives, most likely we will see that no one has ever been there for us in a totally reliable, continuous way. Though we might like to imagine that somebody, somewhere—maybe movie stars or spiritual people—has an ideal relationship, this is mostly the stuff of fantasy. Looking more closely, we can see that everyone has his or her own fears, blind spots, hidden agendas, insecurities, aggressive and manipulative tendencies, and emotional trigger-points—which block the channels through which great love can freely flow. Much as we might want to love with a pure heart, our limitations inevitably cause our love to fluctuate and waver.

Yet our yearning for perfect love and perfect union does have its place and its own beauty. Arising out of an intuitive knowing of the perfection that lies within the heart, it points toward something beyond what ordinary mortals can usually provide. We yearn to heal our separation from life, from God, from our own heart. When understood correctly, this longing can inspire us to reach beyond ourselves, give ourselves wholeheartedly, or turn toward the life of the spirit. It is a key, as we shall see, that opens the doorway through which absolute love can enter fully into us.

We invariably fall into trouble, however, when we transfer this longing onto another person. That is why it's important to distinguish between absolute and relative love—so we don't go around seeking perfect love from imperfect situations. Although intimate connections can provide dazzling flashes of absolute oneness, we simply cannot count on them for that. The only reliable source of perfect love is that which is perfect—the open, awake heart at the core of being. This alone allows us to know perfect union, where all belongs to us because we belong to all. Expecting this from relationships only sets us up to feel betrayed, disheartened, or aggrieved.

The Genesis of the Wound

Riding the waves of relationship becomes particularly difficult when the troughs of misunderstanding, disharmony, or separation reactivate our core wound, bringing up old frustration and hurt from childhood. In the first few months of our life, our parents most likely gave us the largest dose of unconditional love and devotion they were capable of. We were so adorable as babies, they probably felt blessed to have such a precious, lovely being come into their lives. So if we were fortunate enough to have a mother who could care for us at all—a "good enough" mother—we probably had some initial experiences of basking in love's pure, unfiltered sunshine.

When held in the loving arms of their mother, babies relax into the blissful current of warmth that is love as it flows freely through them from the absolute source of all. The mother's caring is the outer condition that lets the child experience the love and joy that is the essence of its own being. When the mother's love is present, the infant can soften and settle into its very own nature as warmth and openness.

Neuropsychology research reveals that the mother-infant bond fosters the infant's development in a number of important ways. At first the mother's physical presence and care help the baby learn to soothe and regulate its nervous system. Healthy maternal attachment also fosters the child's cognitive, behavioral, and somatic development. And it directly affects the development of the limbic brain, with its capacities for interpersonal and emotional responsiveness. Even the health of the endocrine and immune systems is correlated with early maternal attachment or the lack thereof.

Infants experience their mother's presence, and the way her care regulates their nervous system, as something much more tangible and concrete than their connection to the ground of their own being. Since the maternal bond plays such a crucial role in every aspect of the infant's development, it's not surprising that children come to see their mother as the very source of love itself, and in some parts of the world, such as India, as something close to a deity.

Yet this also gives rise to one of the most fundamental of all human illusions: that the source of happiness and well-being lies outside us, in other people's acceptance, approval, or caring. As a child, this was indeed the case, since we were at first so entirely dependent on others for our very life. Under ideal circumstances, the parents' love would gradually become internalized, allowing us to feel our own inner connection to love. But the less experience we have of being loved as we are, the less we feel at home in our own heart. And this leaves us looking to others for the most essential connection of all—with the native sense of rightness and joy that arises only out of being rooted in ourselves.

As the child develops into a separate person, the early blissful moments of oneness with the mother fade away. We are no longer this amazing little being who dropped in from outer space. Instead, for our parents, we become "their child," an object of their hopes and fears. Their acceptance and support become conditional on our meeting their expectations. And this undermines our trust: in ourselves, that we are acceptable as we are; in others, that they can see and value us for who we are; and in love itself, that it is reliably there for us.

Even if at the deepest level our parents did love us unconditionally, it was impossible for them to express this consistently, given their human limitations. This was not their fault. It doesn't mean they were bad parents or bad people. Like everyone, they had their share of fears, worries, cares, and burdens, as well as their own wounding around love. Like all of us, they were imperfect vessels for perfect love.

In entering this world, children naturally want to feel greeted by an unconditional yes and grow up in that kind of environment. This is perfectly understandable. Yet even if parents can provide this to some extent, most often they cannot sustain it. This is also perfectly understandable, since everyone has difficulty remaining open and saying yes to themselves and their life. Being able to sustain an unconditional yes is a highly advanced human capacity that usually develops only through dedicated intention or spiritual practice. Our parents' inability to be fully open naturally limited their capacity to transmit unconditional love to us.

Yet when children experience love as conditional or unreliable or manipulative, this causes a knot of fear to form in the heart, for they can only conclude, "I am not truly loved." This creates a state of panic or "freak-out" that causes the body and mind to freeze up. This basic love trauma is known as "narcissistic injury" in the language of psychotherapy because it damages our sense of self and our ability to feel good about ourselves. It affects our whole sense of who we are by causing us to doubt whether our nature is lovable. As Emily Dickinson describes this universal wound in one of her poems: "There is a pain so utter, it swallows Being up."

This wounding hurts so much that children try to push it out of consciousness. Eventually a psychic scab forms. That scab is our grievance. Grievance against others serves a defensive function, by hardening us so we don't have to experience the underlying pain of not feeling fully loved. And so we grow up with an isolated, disconnected ego, at the core of which is a central wound, freak-out, and shutdown. And all of this is covered over with some resentment, which becomes a major weapon in our defense arsenal.

What keeps the wound from healing is not knowing that we are lovely and lovable just as we are, while imagining that other people hold the key to this. We would like, and often expect, relative human love to be absolute, providing a reliable, steady flow of attunement, unconditional acceptance, and understanding. When this doesn't happen, we take it personally, regarding this as someone's fault—our own, for not being good enough, or others', for not loving us enough. But the imperfect way our parents—or anyone else—loved us has nothing to do with whether love is trustworthy or whether we are lovable. *It doesn't have the slightest bearing on who we really are.* It is simply a sign of ordinary human limitation, and nothing more. Other people cannot love us any more purely than their character structure allows.

Searching for the Source of Love

Fortunately, the storminess of our relationships in no way diminishes or undermines the unwavering presence of great love, absolute love, which is ever present in the background. Even when the sky is filled with thick, dark clouds, the sun never stops shining.

This isn't how it usually appears, of course. Love's radiant presence often seems lost behind clouds of hurt, misunderstanding, disenchantment, and betrayal. Even though the sun is infinitely more powerful than any cloud cover, the overcast does manage to temporarily block its warming rays. This is relative truth—how things appear to the ego when disconnected from its essential foundation, the ground of openness and loving presence. Yet the larger, absolute truth is that the sun never wanes or flickers. It only *appears* to flicker when clouds pass across its face.

This is why it is helpful to look more closely and see what actually happens within us when we feel loved by others. One middle-aged woman I was seeing in therapy was obsessed with winning other people's approval and admiration—so much so that she would literally make herself sick striving and straining to prove herself to others, while worrying about potential loss of esteem in their eyes. One day I asked Anna what actually happened in her body in moments when she managed to win approval or praise.

"I feel great," Anna said.

"And exactly how does that feel in your body? Check it out."

"I relax. I feel bigger somehow," she said, lifting and stretching her elbows behind her head.

"Where in your body do you feel that relaxation and expansion most strongly?"

"Right here," she said, lowering her arms and circling one hand around the center of her chest.

"In your heart."

"Yes."

"So when someone appreciates you, this allows you to feel your own heart."

"Yes," she said, smiling broadly.

"Your heart opens."

"Yes."

"Think about it for a minute. You knock yourself out trying to win approval, and when you finally get it, you experience your heart opening and expanding. Even though you're focused on obtaining something from outside you, it's that inner experience that makes you feel so good. So it seems like what you really most want is to feel your own heart."

Having already had a few powerful glimpses of the presence of her heart in our work together, Anna understood this immediately.

"I never saw that before." Anna paused for a moment, then quickly asked, "How can I hold on to this feeling?" Since this was a new realization, she was afraid she would quickly lose it and fall under the old compulsion to find her lovability through others. Since her family hadn't provided a holding environment where she could relax and trust in love, she had learned early on that she could only get what she needed through trying to please. A go-getter ego had developed precociously in her, supplanting her young girl's heart. Abandoning her heart, she started to live instead from her busy, overactive mind. So it was not surprising that the moment she felt her heart, she started trying to figure out how to hold on to it with her mind.

I encouraged Anna instead to let the realization sink in— that it was the expansive warmth and openness of her heart that she most wanted and that winning approval was merely a means to that end. Learning to recognize this longing for her own heart helped her start to shift her orientation from grasping at love outside to finding love within.

In the same way, you might take a moment and notice how feeling loved allows you to connect with something rich and powerful in yourself. When someone shows you love, it's not that this person is handing something over to you. What really happens is that a window opens inside you, allowing great love to enter and touch you. Another's openness inspires the window of your heart to open, and then love becomes available, *as your own inner experience. This* is what turns you on—this sense of expansive warmth illuminating you from within. Feeling this, you then naturally resonate with the person who is loving you, as you are both sharing in the same experience.

Conversely, if your lover is affectionate at a moment when your heart is burdened by worries, overwhelmed with fear, or frozen shut, you probably won't be able to *feel* his or her love. For love can touch you only when your own heart is accessible. To be loved, then, is to *be* love. The musician Miten describes this experience of landing in the heart in one of his songs:

You gave me the greatest gift:
You made my heart my home.

The problems in relationships begin when we imagine that the warmth ignited in our heart isn't really ours, that it's transferred into us by the other person. Then we become obsessed with the other as the provider of love, when in truth the warmth we feel comes from the sunlight of great love entering our heart.

"Those who go on a search for love," D. H. Lawrence writes, "find only their own lovelessness." Here is a simple way to experience for yourself what Lawrence means. Fix your attention on someone you'd like to love you more, and notice how it feels to want that. If you observe this carefully, you will notice that looking to another for love creates a certain tension or congestion in your body, most noticeably in the chest. It constricts the heart. And as a result you feel your own lovelessness.

No one else can ever provide the connection that finally puts the soul at ease. We find that connection when the window of the heart opens, allowing us to bask in the warmth and openness that is our deepest nature. When we look to others for this ground, we wind up trying to control and manipulate them into being there for us in a way that allows us to settle into ourselves. Yet this very focus on trying to get something from them prevents us from resting in our own ground, leaving us outwardly dependent and inwardly disconnected.

Imagining others to be the source of love condemns us to wander lost in the desert of hurt, abandonment, and betrayal, where human relationship appears to be hopelessly tragic and flawed. Yet hidden within these trials is a certain gift. Our pain at the hands of others forces us to go deeper in search of the true source of love. If other people were perfect vehicles for absolute love, then it would be easy to remain addicted to them as the ultimate source of fulfillment. Becoming totally dependent on others, we would have no incentive to find the great love that is perfectly present within the core of ourselves. We would remain trapped in the consciousness of a child seeking someone to make up for what we didn't receive in childhood.

As long as we fixate on what our parents didn't give us, the ways our friends don't consistently show up for us, or the ways our lover doesn't understand us, we will never become rooted in ourselves and heal the wound of the heart. To grow beyond the dependency of a child requires sinking our own taproot into the wellspring of great love. This is the only way to know for certain that we are loved unconditionally.

In emphasizing the importance of not looking to others for perfect love, I am not suggesting that you turn away from relationships or belittle their importance. On the contrary, learning to sink your taproot into the source of love allows you to connect with others in a more powerful way—"straight up," confidently rooted in your own ground, rather than leaning over, always trying to get something from "out there." The less you demand total fulfillment from relationships, the more you can appreciate them for the beautiful tapestries they are, in which absolute and relative, perfect and imperfect, infinite and finite are marvelously interwoven. You can stop fighting the shifting tides of relative love and learn to ride them instead. And you come to appreciate more fully the simple, ordinary heroism involved in opening to another person and forging real intimacy.

I am also not suggesting that it's impossible to embody absolute, unconditional love in our relationships, for this capacity for selfless caring is surely the greatest and most sacred of all human potentials. But the free flow of love between two intimate partners is usually intermittent at best, since it also inevitably invites the broken, wounded places to step forward into awareness. As that happens and we find ourselves tossed around in the stormy waves of relative love, it can be quite challenging to keep sourcing the pristine love we glimpse in moments of pure opening.

Perhaps only enlightened saints and buddhas can be perfect vessels through which absolute love flows unobstructedly. As a total, unconditional openness to everything that life brings, spiritual awakening allows the heart to become a perfectly clear channel. And this enables the awakened one to keep giving even when the world gives nothing back. Arnaud Desjardins, a French spiritual teacher whose journey began by filming great spiritual masters of the East, searched most of his life for the perfect love that would set him free. Finally he found it, but in an unexpected place. Not where he sought it originally—in the arms of young women—but at the feet of old men—the sages in whose company he sat.

Loving Our Humanness

Yet though perhaps only saints and buddhas embody absolute love completely, nonetheless, every moment of working with the challenges of relative human love brings a hint of this divine possibility into our life. As the child of heaven and earth, you are a mix of infinite openness and finite limitation. This means that you are both wonderful and difficult at the same time. You are flawed, you are stuck in old patterns, you become carried away with yourself. Indeed, you are quite impossible in many ways. *And still,* you are beautiful beyond measure. For the core of what you are is fashioned out of love, that potent blend of openness, warmth, and clear, transparent presence. Boundless love always manages somehow to sparkle through your limited form.

George Orwell once wrote that the essence of being human lies not in seeking perfection but in being "prepared in the end to be defeated and broken up by life, which is the inevitable price of fastening one's love upon other human individuals," who are just as impossible as we are. Orwell is of course describing the poignant, bittersweet quality of relative love. Human relationships often seem utterly impossible because they never seem to fit our ideals and expectations. Again and again they force us to face heartbreak and defeat, until finally the only alternative is to let ourselves be broken up, so that we may remain more open and loving in the face of life as it is.

Bringing absolute love into human form involves learning to hold the impossibility of ourselves and others in the way that the sky holds clouds—with gentle spaciousness and equanimity. The sky can do this because its openness is so much vaster than the clouds that it doesn't find them the least bit threatening. Holding our imperfections in this way allows us to see them as trail markers of the work-in-progress that we are, rather than as impediments to love or happiness. Then we can say, "Yes, everyone has relative weaknesses that cause suffering, yet everyone also possesses absolute beauty, which far surpasses these limitations. Let us melt down the frozen, fearful places by holding them in the warmth of tenderness and mercy."

In his book *Works of Love,* the Danish philosopher Søren Kierkegaard points out that true love doesn't embrace others *in spite of* their flaws, as if rising above them. Rather, it finds "the other lovable in spite of *and together with* his weaknesses and errors and imperfections. . . . Because of your beloved's weakness you shall not remove yourself from him or make your relationship more remote; on the contrary, the two of you shall hold together with greater solidarity and inwardness in order to remove the weakness."

The same holds true for loving yourself. When you recognize that the absolute beauty within you cannot be tarnished by your flaws, then this beauty you are can begin to care for the beast you sometimes seem to be. Beauty's touch begins to soften the beast's gnarly defenses.

Then you begin to discover that the beast and the beauty go hand in hand. The beast is, in fact, nothing other than your wounded beauty. It is the beauty that has lost faith in itself because it has never been fully recognized. Not trusting that you are loved or lovable has given rise to all the most beastly emotional reactions—anger, arrogance, hatred, jealousy, meanness, depression, insecurity, greedy attachment, fear of loss and abandonment.

While the beast has a certain limited power—to say no and shut down in self-defense—it is cut off from a much greater power, the capacity to say yes. Just as the dancer's grace lies in yielding, bending, and flowing with every pulse of the music, this is also how our beauty reveals itself—in our capacity to open to reality and ride on life's swiftly changing currents. The wounded beast is only the shutting down of that marvelous capacity for grace and fluidity.

The first step in freeing the beast from its burden is to acknowledge the hardening around our heart. Then, peering behind this barrier, we may encounter the wounded, cut-off place in ourselves where the mood of unlove resides. If we can meet this place gently, without judgment or rejection (and chapters 3 and 4 will concretely demonstrate how to do this), we will uncover the great tenderness that resides at the very core of our humanness.

Our beauty and our beast both arise from one and the same tenderness. When we harden against it, the beast is born. Yet when we allow the tenderness, we begin to discern the contours of a long-lost beauty hidden within the belly of the beast. If we can shine warmth and openness into the dark, tender place where we don't know we're lovable, this starts to forge a marriage between our beauty and our wounded beast.

This is, after all, the love we most long for—this embracing of our humanness, which lets us appreciate ourselves as the beautiful, luminous beings we are, housed in a vulnerable, flickering form whose endless calling is to move from chrysalis to butterfly, from seed to new birth. As earthly creatures continually subject to relative disappointment, pain, and loss, we cannot avoid feeling vulnerable. Yet as an open channel through which great love enters this world, the human heart remains invincible. Being wholly and genuinely human means standing firmly planted in both dimensions, celebrating that we are both vulnerable and indestructible at the same time.

Here at this crossroads where yes and no, limitless love and human limitation, intersect, we discover the essential human calling: progressively unveiling the sun in our heart, that it may embrace the whole of ourselves and the whole of creation within the sphere of its radiant warmth. This love is not the least bit separate from true power. For, as the great Sufi poet Rumi sings:

When we have surrendered totally to that beauty,
Then we shall be a mighty kindness.

CHAPTER TWO

The Mood of Grievance

Who is it that's unhappy?
The one who finds fault.

—ANONYMOUS

THE MOST DESTRUCTIVE element in human relationships is the urge to make other people bad or wrong, and then judge, reject, or punish them for that. The tragic consequences of this show up everywhere: in feuds within marriages, families, and organizations; wars between nations; and constant strife between people who are unable to accept one another's differences. The long-standing conflicts in the Middle East have this character, where the intensity of the grudges and the urge to retaliate have developed a momentum that keeps escalating far beyond where it has the slightest benefit for anyone.

The suicide bomber expresses the mind-set of grievance in an especially intense way. Most of us probably find it hard to understand how anyone could value his life so little that he is willing to blow himself up in order to get back at those who have wronged him or his people. Yet if we look closer, we can find the makings of a suicide bomber within each one of us.

Nursing a grievance—treating our intimate partner as someone to get back at, or resenting how badly life or other people have treated us—is a self-destructive act. For in wanting to hurt or reject someone or something we resent, we unwittingly wind up hurting or rejecting ourselves at the same time. This is easy to see: just notice how your whole body tightens and constricts when you hold something against someone. When you do this, you are destroying your own life—the presence, openness, and warmth that is your lifeblood. So to make the other bad at the expense of feeling good ourselves is to choose death over life, just like the suicide bomber.

This is one of the most striking phenomena I observe in working with couples: how they often have much more energy for making each other wrong than for setting things right between them. They often have tremendous investment in their complaint: "You did this to me; you said that to me. You have wronged me." Some people are so deeply wedded to their grievance that they are willing to blow up the relationship and their own happiness just to prove that their partner is wrong and they are right.

Grievance at Work

Dan and Nancy were a case in point. After five years of marriage, Nancy had amassed a large collection of grievances against Dan, based on her hurt about not feeling fully loved. Dan was certainly not the most responsive lover and husband. But Nancy also seemed to take perverse pleasure in holding his sins of omission and commission against him. It was as though she kept a running tally and were continually saying, "See, there you go again. You just proved once again that you don't really love me. If you really loved me, you would have: paid closer attention . . . listened more carefully . . . called me . . . apologized . . . acknowledged me more in public . . . not looked at any other woman in the room . . . not raised your voice. . . ."

To Dan, Nancy's list of grievances seemed endless. Each time he did something that provided fresh evidence that "he didn't really love her," Nancy would pull out her list to seal the case. Dan felt he didn't stand a chance, because every time he did something "right," it could never measure up against the long list of his recorded wrongs. So he gradually lost interest in trying. While he certainly had difficulty being attentive to others' needs, he did care about Nancy and wanted to make her happy. But out of frustration about never being able to do enough for her, he had hardened into the position that she was simply impossible.

When this couple first came in, they were like two prosecuting attorneys trying to prove just how wrong the other was. Nancy was firm in her righteous grievance, while Dan was steadfast in his complaint that Nancy would never be happy with him, no matter how hard he tried. Since most of their relational energy went into the battle between their two grievance positions, there was little energy left over for trying to move in a new direction. This kind of standoff is common in marriage and long-term relationships.

Some would argue that this kind of adversarial bitterness shows that human beings are basically aggressive, or that war is more fundamental than love in human relations. But I see it the other way around. Just as a clenched fist is possible only because of the open hand that precedes it, so war and aggression are not primary, but a shutting down of our more fundamental openness. They are what we do when we feel wounded or insecure, that is, cut off from love. Similarly, just as the sky can hold clouds but clouds cannot hold the vast expanse of the sky, so love is greater than hatred because it can embrace hatred, while hatred cannot embrace love. While love can exist free of hatred, hatred exists only because of love, as a painful symptom of our disconnection from it.

So if love is primary, why then is war so prominent in human relationships and world affairs? The answer lies in unpacking the phenomenon of grievance. Grievance is the missing link between love and war: Peace degenerates into war and honeymoons lead to divorces through the reenactment of old grievances.

Unpacking Grievance

Most of us are unaware of how invested we are in grievance and how much it governs our life. To set things right in this world and allow love to occupy its rightful place at the center of our life, we need to bring the mood of grievance into the full light of awareness. We need to recognize how much we hold on to grudges—and to understand why. We need to see how grievance works and what function it serves. In this way we begin to unpack grievance, opening up the tight, dark corner that it occupies within us. And this starts to remove the grime that has formed on the window of the heart, so that love's clear light can enter in more fully.

Every grievance has its roots in old hurt about not being fully loved and old frustration about not being able to do anything about that. Once established, this hurt and frustration become like a hidden virus that remains dormant in our nervous system, ready to flare up the moment someone looks at us the wrong way. This is what triggers all the emotional eruptions that afflict our relationships.

So rather than concluding that human beings are basically belligerent, we need instead to understand exactly why we hold on to these old grievances that underlie all our acts of aggression. What is clear is that holding in mind what has hurt us in the past is a survival mechanism, a way of trying to make sure it won't creep up on us again while we're off guard. The mind holding on to grievance is like a full-time sentry guard whose job is to remain on the lookout for emotional threats from other people. Simply put, we don't want to be wounded again, like we were before, once long ago.

Most of the time the sentry quietly goes about his patrol and we're not even aware he's on duty. But then when someone crosses us, slights us, ignores or hurts us, the alarm bells go off. As this alarm runs through our nervous system, it triggers an upsurge of charged emotion. And then we swing into some aggressive or defensive maneuver—anger, blame, attack, withdrawal, or flight—to fend off this threat.

A less dramatic, more recurring symptom of grievance at work is our perpetual tendency to judge other people. Have you ever noticed how many judgmental or blaming thoughts pass through your mind every hour of every day? Usually it's hard to be aware of just how many judgments we have of others unless we slow down and observe the mind more carefully. The first words out of the mouth of an eighteen-year-old I know, at the conclusion of her first silent meditation retreat, were: "I never realized before just how judgmental I was!"

Why all these judgmental thoughts? Standing in judgment of others is a way to feel superior, by placing ourselves above them. Yet why on earth would we need to feel superior unless we also somehow felt inferior deep within and were trying to compensate for that? Judging others allows me to feel right-eous and one up, which shields me from the pain of their judgment and rejection of me. In judging them, I neutralize their power over me. So here again we see the wound at work: Judging and condemning others is an attempt to avoid experiencing the pain and fear of not feeling loved.

And so our judgmental thoughts arrive like automatic in-terest payments that we continually receive on our invest-ment in grievance. Unfortunately, they take us away from being right here in the present, the only place where real love and happiness can happen. The mind that scans the environ-ment for threats, insults, and things we don't like keeps us edgy and tense, preventing us from opening up and letting love in.

The Bad Other

An important step in releasing ourselves from the grip of grievance is to recognize the linchpin that holds it in place: *the fixation on the "bad other."* The bad other is our internal image of the one who doesn't love us or treat us well. It can be seen operating in our tendency to be on the lookout for wrongs di-rected at us. Unless we bring this inner image to conscious-ness and see how much we focus on other people as potential threats, this tendency will operate unconsciously, forever poi-soning our relations with others.

Let's look at how the bad-other image forms in the mind. As young children we totally depended on our parents for everything. When receiving our mother's care, we formed a sense of the "good mother" within us. Yet since no mother can ever be totally attuned to her child, we also had experiences of a mother who neglected, frustrated, or hurt us.

Young children have no way to comprehend how a parent can be "good," a source of pleasure and happiness, one minute, and "bad," a source of pain and frustration, the next. It requires a great deal of maturity to hold a balanced, nuanced picture of other people that includes both their pleasing and unpleasant qualities. If children had this maturity, they might be able to say to themselves: "I'm feeling neglected right now, but I can see that my mother is having a hard time. She is burdened and pressured herself. She has had a hard life, and having a young child is bringing up all of her own unresolved conflicts and needs. So the fact that she can't be there for me right now doesn't mean anything bad about her or about me." If children were capable of that kind of understanding, there would be no need for psychotherapists!

Since young children are so totally dependent on their parents, they need to see them as good. Seeing the parents as bad would undermine the child's sense of safety and security. So children usually drop their experience of the frustrating, hurtful mother out of awareness, and it falls into the shadow of unconsciousness (from whence it emerges in fairy tales as the wicked witch or evil stepmother, or on the male side, as the malevolent giant or ogre). This is how children protect their connection with the good mother—the one who feeds and cares for them—and maintain their equilibrium.

But whenever any aspect of our experience falls into unconsciousness, it takes on a life of its own, growing in the darkness like mold silently spreading through a basement. Thus the repressed sense of the frustrating or neglectful parent eventually blossoms into a more generalized sense of the *bad other*—the other who cannot love you as you are, who threatens to hurt or betray you and therefore cannot be trusted. In this way, the bad other takes up permanent residence in the shadows of the mind.

This explains one of the most disturbing and perplexing experiences that crop up in intimate relationships: One moment two lovers can feel sweet and loving, and then, with the exchange of but a few words, they can be at each other's throats. How can the honeymoon glow of new love dissolve so quickly into mutual acrimony and recrimination? How can two people who claim to love each other more than anyone else in the world turn against each other so suddenly, reacting with violent aggression or fright, as though they were the worst of enemies? This instant enmity has shaken many a lover into wondering whether he or she has gone stark, raving mad or whether the beloved is actually a Jekyll-Hyde monster. What is even more mystifying is that these flare-ups are often triggered by the most trivial incidents, such as a partner's showing up ten minutes late.

These explosions of rage and blame happen when the bad-other image and its painful associations suddenly emerge into consciousness and become projected on the one we love. It's as though our full-time security guard keeps a Most Wanted Criminal poster on the wall and is constantly scanning the environment for signs of this villain. So whenever our partner acts, speaks, or treats us in a way that even slightly fits this profile, it triggers a deeply submerged sense of alarm, and we shift into fighting for all we're worth.

Suddenly we see those we care about as the living embodiment of everyone who has ever hurt or rejected us: "I knew I never should have trusted you. You're just like all the rest. I'll show you that you can't treat me like this." And even worse, as we retaliate with blame or aggression, this sets off our partner's alarms. He or she then reacts to us in turn with defensiveness or aggression, which further justifies our bad-other story. And the conflict escalates from there.

A woman has had a stressful day at work, and that evening happens to be the time her lover chooses to reach out to her in a highly intimate way. When she doesn't respond in the way he had hoped, he sees her as an embodiment of all the unresponsive people in his life, starting with his mother, who were too caught up in their own world to show interest in him. So he suddenly goes cold and says something nasty. He has become so swept up in reactive emotion that he doesn't realize he's not even seeing his partner; instead, he's projecting an image of the bad other onto her, based on his old wound. In truth, she may care deeply about him and their potential for greater intimacy. But he can't see that right now because his ancient bad-other picture is occupying the screen of his awareness.

Road rage is another common instance of how old grievances against the bad other can spring to life full-blown at a moment's notice. Why else would perfectly nice people suddenly turn into monsters behind the wheel? The faceless driver who cuts in front of you represents everyone who hasn't treated you with caring or kindness. And as you lean on the horn or yell obscenities, you want to let this person know you're not going to take it anymore.

A therapist I know told a funny story about driving to work and taking a parking space that another driver coming from the other direction had been eyeing. The other driver started honking his horn and then leaned out the window to make an obscene gesture, when he suddenly saw that the person he was yelling at was his therapist. Needless to say, they had an interesting session that afternoon.

Modern warfare, like road rage, is another vehicle for en-acting ancient grievances about feeling mistreated. Especially when war is waged with technology, with little person-to-person contact, it becomes easy to project the bad other onto an enemy people that have no face. In demonizing the enemy, war draws popular support from the grievance mentality smoldering in the populace at large. What underlies all the war rhetoric is: "I don't feel important; I don't feel properly recognized, honored, or respected. I haven't been given my due. I'm angry about that, and I'm going to show those bastards they can't push me around." In belligerence against other nations, a people may use bombs and missiles to com-pensate for a deep sense of powerlessness, helplessness, and frustration that, if we trace it all the way back, is rooted in the wound of the heart.

In personal relationships, subconscious bad-other images cause people to overemphasize and overreact to the ways their partner is not attuned to them, while minimizing or overlooking the ways the other does love or care for them. Often there is one aggrieved partner who tends to complain, while the browbeaten partner tends to withdraw to ward off the onslaught. This was what was happening with Dan and Nancy.

After years of defending himself against Nancy's com-plaint that he didn't love her, Dan learned through our work together to show up and be more attentive and present with her. I have witnessed this countless times—the withdrawn partner finally coming forward to meet the aggrieved partner in a beautiful fresh moment that I often find quite moving. I sit there feeling, "Wow, that's so great. He [she] finally took the risk and showed up." But then, to my dismay, the ag-grieved partner hardly seems to notice!

Once when Dan made himself emotionally available to Nancy, she held firmly to her grievance: "I don't trust this. I can't imagine it will last when we leave your office." While her concern was understandable, she was also bringing it up in a way that kept Dan at bay, thereby justifying her complaint.

This is what is tragic about the mood of grievance: It shuts down the channel through which love could enter into us, cutting us off from its healing and regenerative power. In one way or another, many of us suffer from the same problem as Nancy: "I don't feel loved" eventually hardens into "I don't trust love enough to let it in." Opening to love feels too threatening, and we don't believe it's safe to do so. The final step in sealing ourselves into this box is to cover up our emotional vulnerability with blame or condemnation: "You don't really love me. . . . You don't know how to love. . . ."

Thus the mood of grievance is totally self-defeating, not only shutting us down to love but also driving others, who are the target of our complaint, away. In treating Dan as the bad other who couldn't be there for her, Nancy triggered his own inner freak-out about being unworthy and unlovable. This brought up shame and self-blame, making it harder for him to be open to her. In that contracted condition, he also had little to give. And the less he could give, the more Nancy felt justified in her grievance. Meanwhile, his bad-other projection on Nancy—that she was impossible—made it harder for her to soften as well. This is how grievances invariably become self-fulfilling prophecies.

One American psychiatrist, Vamik Volkan, has studied how this mind-set operates in certain ethnic groups and nations that define themselves in terms of a victim identity, based on historic wrongs and oppressions. Volkan uses the term "chosen trauma" to describe this phenomenon. Looking at the world through the lens of their chosen trauma, such groups are continually on the lookout for dangers and threats from some other ethnic group. This makes them act in defensive and aggressive ways that generate fear and animosity in the other group, which then reacts in hostile ways, thereby confirming the first group's view of the world as unfriendly.

In a similar way, we all harbor our own chosen trauma—about not getting enough love. And our story about the bad other who has wronged and deprived us generates fear, suspicion, resentment, distrust, or aggression that inevitably pushes others away and undermines our relationships, thereby reconfirming the old belief that we're not loved or lovable. Thus we keep reenacting the child's original love trauma by continually generating fresh evidence that the world is indeed a loveless place.

Grievance Run Amok

One of the most insidious things about grievance is that it takes on a life of its own and poisons everything, cutting us off from the joy and beauty of life. What started out as a hurt feeling turns into a generalized grudge against the world.

My mother provided me with an up-close study in how grievance becomes generalized into a whole way of being. Although she had a big heart and was basically very kind and generous, she had had a very hard childhood, and as she grew older, she began to dwell in grievance as a way of life. In the last half of her life, she always had something to complain vociferously about, whether it was politicians, the weather, the food she ate, her relatives, her doctors, or the apartment in which she lived. At a moment's notice she would launch into long, bitter tirades about any of these things. At these times there was no reasoning with her, and she would brush aside any of my attempts to provide a more balanced, less negative view of things.

Toward the end of her life, when she was being taken care of by home health aides, many of whom were immigrants, she would complain about how awful it was that there were so many immigrants in America. Yet whenever one of them showed up to help, she was actually quite kind and sweet to them. There was one Jamaican woman whom my mother was particularly fond of and grateful toward. I saw that in the moment of relating to someone personally, her heart could be present in a direct, pure way, even though at other times she might include these same people in her tirades against the bad other. Grievance had become so woven into her identity and psyche that it had taken on a life of its own, remaining split off from her awareness and even from her actual behavior.

In observing my mother, as well as the tendencies I inherited from her, I saw how grievance can take on a life of its own. It doesn't matter whom the grudge is directed toward, because the target can change with the circumstances; it becomes a "movable grievance." A few years before my mother formed her grievance against immigrants, she had one against gays and lesbians, and people on welfare before that, and men with long hair before that. As grievance generalizes, it finally becomes a complaint about the way things are and The Injustice Of It All, which winds up isolating us from life altogether.

The Investment in Grievance

Given that grievance exacts such a heavy toll, what makes it so compelling and hard to let go of? Wanting to explore this more fully, I brought this question to the students in my group the week following their exploration of how the stress in their lives was based in old grievances arising out of their core wound.

"Now that we've looked at the painful and destructive consequences of grievance," I said, "I'd like you to check something else out. See if you are willing to let go of your grievance. Please be honest. Who's willing to do that right now?" There was silence. Not a single person raised a hand! I said, "Good. Thank you for your honesty. Before we can find a way to let our grievances go, it's essential to acknowledge how attached we are to them. We need to understand our whole investment in grievance and see exactly why we hold on to it so tightly."

I then asked them to pair up and explore with each other what was good about holding on to grievance. In other words, what purpose did it serve, what was the benefit or pay-off it provided, what did they get out of maintaining it? Here are some of the answers people came up with.

"Holding on to my grievance gives me a sense of power, which protects me from feeling vulnerable. It's a way of standing up for myself and defending myself from being hurt, disappointed, or rejected again. It keeps me vigilant against recurrences of harm."

"Holding on to a grudge lets me feel right and right-eous. It's as if I have my own private jihad. Giving it up would be a way of letting the people who hurt me off the hook and letting them walk all over me."

"Grievance bolsters a familiar sense of 'me'—I know myself in this place. It gives me a sense of identity. Even though it doesn't actually feel good, I'd rather live with this familiar discomfort than let the grievance go and feel the discomfort of stepping into the unknown. Letting it go would undermine my whole identity."

"It's a way of saying 'poor me' and feeling sorry for myself. So it becomes a way of trying to get some sympathy. It's a cry for help."

"Holding on to a grievance is a way of taking care of myself, of soothing myself by shifting my attention away from the wound. In this sense, it's self-affirming."

"It's a way of bonding with the members of my family, who all harbor some complaint against the world. My family were immigrants who were mistreated in Europe for many generations and again when they first arrived in America. Voicing our grievances is a way of licking our wounds together. Being victims together is a membership card in the family."

"It provides an organizing principle—a unifying story about exploitation, oppression, haves versus have-nots, and fighting to get what you need—which gives me a worldview, a sense of what I need to fight for. This provides a sense of order and purpose in the midst of chaos."

"My grievance is bound up with feelings of being abandoned by my father, who left our family when I was young. Oddly enough, holding on to it helps me maintain some emotional connection with him. I can see how my anger and resentment are a way of trying to hold on to him."

"Shifting the blame onto others allows me not to have to take responsibility for my own problems."

No wonder it's so hard to let go of our grievance and forgive. These statements show the powerful functions it can serve in the psyche. If we have a grievance ready at hand, it can protect us from feeling vulnerable. We can avoid putting ourselves in situations like the one that originally hurt us. Hardening around grievance gives us a certain righteous strength: "I'll show you that you can't mess with me. I'll show you I'm someone to be reckoned with." It seems to provide a place to stand.

Furthermore, as a way of making others bad or wrong, grievance is also a way of trying to feel better about ourselves. That was why my mother indulged in complaining about people whom she actually liked in person. Complaining about the bad other let her feel righteous, and thus good about herself. Criticizing others' faults was a way she could access some power, to compensate for how small and helpless she felt inside. It gave her a sense of being somebody in a world where she felt totally at sea.

All of this sheds light on why it is often hard to let ourselves receive love even when it's available. *To let love in requires us to melt*—to dissolve our hardened defenses and let down our guard. Receiving love is more threatening than giving it because receptivity requires opening, which feels vulnerable. So even though we may cry out for love, as Nancy did with Dan, when love is actually available, we often sabotage the relationship, shut down in fear, or provoke a conflict that will justify our grievance. Then we can feel safe again, righteously justifying our shutdown as a way to protect ourselves from the bad other.

No wonder nations so quickly demand an eye for an eye and march off to war to settle disputes. If we as individuals are not ready to give up our personal grievances, how can we condemn our leaders for waging war, since we nurture the same seeds of violence within ourselves? To the extent that we indulge in the mood of grievance, each of us is implicated in the strife that dominates our planet.

This is why Jesus's injunction to turn the other cheek is such an important teaching: It strikes at the heart of the grievance mentality, which is the core of the defensive ego, around which our sense of identity and security is built.

When I present these ideas about grievance in workshops, people often ask, "What about legitimate grievances that have to be addressed, such as social injustice or oppression, or abusive relationships?" Certainly there are legitimate wrongs and injustices that require attention and action. However, if we come from the mood of grievance, insisting on our virtue while condemning the badness of those who wrong us, we are unlikely to address these concerns in a constructive way that leads to true peace and justice.

The Dalai Lama, for example, has as much to be aggrieved about as anyone in the world. As the exiled leader of Tibet, which was brutally invaded and occupied by China in the 1950s, he has witnessed the desecration and destruction of all that he held most dear: his people, his culture, the free practice of his religion, and the land and wildlife of Tibet. The Chinese occupation has been responsible for the torture and murder of up to two million Tibetans, and this living holocaust continues to this day.

The Dalai Lama has worked tirelessly to redress this situation, but he has made a choice not to live in a mind-state of grievance, bitterness, or resentment. Far from it, he lives and breathes joy and directs compassion toward the Chinese invaders, out of concern for the great harm they are doing themselves by acting so hatefully. He knows that the mood of grievance confers no benefit whatsoever, for himself or for anyone else. And he makes an all-important distinction: He recognizes evil actions without regarding the people who perform them as intrinsically bad. He understands that people are usually unconscious and therefore helpless in the face of the karmic forces that propel their hurtful behavior. His understanding accords with that of Jesus's words on the Cross: "Father, forgive them, for they know not what they do."

No doubt the Dalai Lama's great popularity stems from his living embodiment of Christ's injunction to turn the other cheek. Although few of us possess this level of strength and courage, nonetheless the Dalai Lama's example shows us that human beings can conduct themselves with great dignity in the face of horrendous suffering and injustice.

After my students finished exploring their personal investment in grievance, I asked them to acknowledge their unwillingness to let it go and see what that felt like. A few people judged themselves harshly for this, but they could also see that this was just another form of grievance—against themselves. Most of the others felt a sense of relief—about seeing the truth. As one woman put it: "It makes me feel hopeful. Seeing how I'm so invested in grievance gives me a concrete sense of what I need to work on in myself. And I see how important that is if I want to have real freedom and love in my life. Understanding this opens up whole new possibilities."

CHAPTER THREE

Letting Grievance Go

I was born when all I once feared
I could love.
—Rabia

The heart is itself its own medicine. The
heart all its own wounds heals.
—Hazrat Inayat Khan

How can we free ourselves from the mood of grievance, which only serves to perpetuate the wound of love by reinforcing fear and resentment of others? There is a powerful teaching from the Tantric traditions of India and Tibet that can help us here: *The medicine can be found within the poison.* If grievance is like poison, this teaching suggests that the cure lies in the grievance itself. So instead of looking outside ourselves for something to blame, we need to be willing to look within and to face what lies there, in the heart of the grievance.

What lies at the core of all grievance is deep pain and grief about loss of connection. Because we have never fully and consciously grieved this hurt, it becomes coagulated in our mind and body. *What we fail to grieve turns into grievance.* To extract the medicine that can heal the poison of grievance, we need to acknowledge and allow this grief, instead of running away from it. This means bringing our grief about loss of connection out of the shadows into the daylight of openness and warmth.

Melting Grievance into Grief

At first, of course, we do not know that our hurt is bearable. No one has ever modeled for us how to bear pain in a strong, dignified, or fruitful way. So the automatic reaction is to deny our grief and fashion a cool facade to cover it up. Yet behind the facade, there lies a simple truth, a running sore, a wound we share with billions of other people on this planet: We don't know in our bones that we are loved or lovable, that reality is ultimately benevolent, or that great love is the ground of our whole existence.

To turn away from our hurt is to abandon and thus re-wound ourselves. The only way to heal the wound of the heart is through freeing up the feelings about loss of connection that remain stored in our body, so that they can be fully digested and move on through us. We first experienced loss of connection in relation to our parents, then again with friends who turned away, lovers who lost interest, or a husband or wife who shut down or left. Yet deeper still is the loss of connection with ourselves that happens when we spurn our own hurt, confusion, or despair. This creates inner division and discord that prevent us from fully recognizing our intrinsic beauty and lovability and establishing a blessed connection with ourselves.

I am not suggesting that you must go through an elaborate grieving catharsis for your past losses, though that might be helpful for some. What is most important is to acknowledge the truth—your separation from love, and the pain of that— and to open your heart to yourself in the place of unlove. Learning to hold your woundedness in the embrace of your own compassionate presence helps you be present to yourself in a new way that penetrates the thick, defensive shell around the heart. This is what allows the medicine to flow.

Meeting Yourself in the Place of Unlove

How to hold your pain in a way that heals? The two dimensions of holding discussed earlier are important here: making contact and giving space, letting be. To illustrate how this works, I will draw on a condensed example of work with one of my psychotherapy clients. Jane's situation and feelings were classic, and the sequence she moved through was also fairly typical. Following along with this example will help you start to see how you can work with your own wounding in a similar way.

Jane was with a man who was not sure he wanted to continue the relationship, and his ambivalence had persisted for more than a year. She very much wanted the relationship, and Tom's ambivalence kept triggering and aggravating her old wound of "I'm not good enough to be loved and wanted." In that wounded place she would lose connection with herself and fixate intensely on Tom—on how he was treating her or on how she could convince him to stay.

Jane spent our first few sessions together laying out her grievances about Tom and describing her childhood experience of not feeling seen or accepted in her family. After we had established a groundwork of trust and understanding, I asked Jane to tune in to her sense of not feeling loved, as she experienced that in her body. At first she could only contact her defensive shell: "I feel shut down and guarded."

When I asked her to see what was under that, she got in touch with her fear and desperation about being left. After working with this for a while, it became clear she was still entirely focused on Tom and what he might do. Jane still hadn't made contact with what was being touched and triggered inside her that made her so fearful and desperate. Eventually she said: "I hate feeling like this."

"Feeling like what?" I asked.

"So unloved."

"How does that feel in your body?" I was inviting her to make direct contact with her bodily felt experience of the pain of feeling unloved. This direct contact is what I call acknowledging. This is the first step of meeting and inhabiting one's experience—a process I call *unconditional presence*. This process can be divided into four closely related steps—acknowledging, allowing, opening, and entering. These steps are a way of defining different moments in a process of ever-greater presence with emotional experience.

Acknowledging means recognizing what is there, recognizing *that it is,* without trying to assess whether it is good or bad, or whether it *should* be this way or not. Seeing and touching a feeling that is there, as it is—this is what I mean by acknowledgment. In my work as a psychotherapist, I have found that this simple act of acknowledgment possesses far greater power than any self-help strategy or mental analysis.

"How does it sit in you right now, the feeling of being unloved?" I asked.

"There's some soreness here," Jane said, touching her chest.

"Can you let the breath touch that soreness? See if you can just let the feeling be there, without trying to fix or change it." I was inviting her to take a further step—to allow the feeling: "See if you can soften around it, holding the soreness very softly and spaciously, like the sky holds the earth." *Allowing* means giving the feeling plenty of space to be there just as it is, while continuing to stay in contact with it.

Often we unconsciously compress or constrict painful feelings as a way of trying to keep them away or make them smaller and less consequential. Allowing is a form of decompression or unstuffing: letting the energy of the feeling be as large as it is, without either identifying with it ("this pain is me, it means something about who I am") or rejecting it ("this pain isn't me, it shouldn't be there"). When Jane could give her pain room to be there, this provided an immediate sense of relief, because she was no longer in a struggle with it. She was meeting and connecting with the wound of love as a simple human feeling rather than as a big melodrama.

Occasionally Jane would drift off into mental judgments or stories about the pain. It is important in this process not to become caught up in these mental interpretations or dramas ("This feeling is too much, it's bigger than I am, it will swallow me alive") because they interfere with meeting your experience directly. This is especially true with harsh judgments ("If I feel so unloved, it means I'm no good"). I helped Jane to recognize these judgments as stories she was telling herself, and then to gently put them aside and come back to sensing the present feeling in her body.

Next I encouraged Jane to see if she could open herself to the painful sense of not feeling loved. *Opening* in this context means opening one's heart to a feeling, letting oneself fully experience the sensations stirring in the body without maintaining any struggle against them. After spending some time opening to the feeling, she said, "I feel more calm. The ache is still there, but I can let it be there." Opening herself to the pain had allowed her to settle down with it, so it no longer felt so threatening.

After a while I invited Jane to go a little further, to enter into the felt sense of unlove and inhabit it fully. *Entering* means bringing one's awareness right into the core of a feeling, so that one is at one with it, no longer seeing it as something apart from oneself. "Can you let your awareness enter into the ache, as if you're moving right into the center of it?"

"It feels really sad and vulnerable," she said.

"Yes. . . . See if you can be one with the sadness; don't remain separate from it. See if you can soften into it."

She fell silent for a few minutes. Eventually she said, "The sadness is still there, but it's not so heavy." In a little while she sat up straight and looked at me. "It's shifting. I still feel the vulnerability, but there's also more tenderness and warmth." Her face had totally relaxed and she was obviously more settled in her body.

"How are you experiencing yourself now?"

"It's strange. . . . There's some sweetness there," she said, with a tentative smile. "With that sweetness there, do you still feel disconnected from love?" I asked. Jane considered this quietly for a while and then said, "Not right now." No longer focused on Tom or their relationship, Jane was feeling her own heart, which ushered her into a lovely sense of sweetness in the body. Meeting herself in the place of unlove and opening to her pain and vulnerability had kindled love within her—as a subtle presence of sweetness and warmth entering into her darkest corners.

What had clouded Jane's access to her own heart was her fear of the pain of unlove and her attempts to convince Tom to stay so she wouldn't have to feel this pain. She now realized that trying so hard to get Tom to love her had only separated her from love by turning it into something that was in his hands to confer upon her. As a result, whenever Tom would turn away, she felt cut off from her very heart. And that disconnect from the blessed flow of love within herself was the greatest heartache of all.

So whenever you feel unloved, instead of looking for some external remedy, you could take this as a sign that you're disconnected from your own heart. That disconnect is the poison. Letting yourself open to the pain of that disconnect puts you in touch with a certain tenderness or vulnerability, which is a signal that your heart, with its natural longing and capacity to connect, is close at hand. This brings you back to yourself—which *is* the medicine for the disconnect. The pain of unlove is thus much more than just pain. It is a direct cry from the heart: "You've lost touch with me, please come and find me, your life's blood."

Of course, feeling unloved is usually the last thing we want to experience, because we associate it with deficiency: isolation, emptiness, shame, or inadequacy. Why on earth, you may wonder, would you want to let yourself feel unloved? Yet if this feeling is there, there are only two choices: avoiding and denying it or facing it directly.

If you flee from the wound, you only give it more power over you. Eventually your emotional body becomes like an abandoned, haunted house. The more you flee the pain of unlove, the more it festers in the dark and the more haunted your house becomes. And the more haunted it becomes, the more it terrifies you. This is the vicious circle that keeps you cut off from and afraid of yourself.

But when you can meet yourself in the place of unlove, this starts to open the doors and windows of the haunted house, letting in sunlight and fresh air. Gradually the house becomes more livable. Through learning to tolerate painful or vulnerable feelings, you develop a new muscle. With your growing capacity to handle your pain, the wound that once seemed so huge, so monstrous, so overwhelming, becomes tolerable.

By *meeting yourself in the place where you feel unmet*, something new and powerful happens. Something so simple yet so radical: *You start to inhabit yourself.* You reinhabit your lonely heart and bring it back to life.

Owning Your Anger or Hatred

Allowing and inhabiting the grief at the core of grievance reconnects us with the feminine tenderness of the heart, releasing healing medicine that softens the hard-heartedness of grievance. Yet there is another resource we also need to tap if we are to stop investing in grievance: masculine power and strength. This power stems from standing in our truth—what is deeply true for us. Standing in this power frees us from regarding others as a threat.

Nursing grievance promotes a certain hardening that masquerades as strength but that actually keeps us in the disempowered victim stance of "they did me wrong." In this mind-state, our strength is locked up in impotent rage and hatred about how we've been treated. Yet there is also potent medicine—vital power and no-nonsense clarity—hidden within the poison of aggression. In order to extract this medicine from the poison, we need to relate to the anger and hatred dwelling within us in a more conscious, deliberate way.

My work with Jane eventually led in this direction. After a few weeks of working with her grief, Jane came in and said, "I notice that I still feel like a victim when Tom doesn't hear me."

"What actually happens inside you when he doesn't hear you?"

"I used to erupt in anger when that happened, but that went nowhere and was too painful. So now I just shut down and become cold."

Freezing like this cut Jane off from her power, keeping her stuck in the victim position. I encouraged her to let her anger come forward, and we worked with it in the way we had with her grief—acknowledging it, giving it plenty of room to be there, and opening to its intense energy.

Making friends with her anger was helpful. But after working with her anger like this, I could also sense a deeper frozenness in her. So I asked her if there was something else there, something more like hatred. At first Jane didn't want to go there, because of a strong moral belief that it was wrong to hate. So we talked about hatred as a feeling, which, like any feeling, is neither right nor wrong in itself. And Jane could see how hatred became particularly problematic when it went underground, where it coagulated and became converted into a toxic story about the bad other.

In a little while Jane said, "Yes, I do hate Tom when he refuses to listen to me." I said, "See if you can feel the energy in the hatred itself, without focusing so much on Tom or what he's doing. Let yourself feel it as an energy, rather than as a grievance story. Give the feeling plenty of breathing room, let it expand and radiate, and see what happens."

After sitting with the energy of hatred in her body and breathing deeply, she began to speak of how she had felt like this when her father would come home from work and not pay attention to her. She recognized how she had taken that personally, imagining she was unworthy of his attention, and how this had left her feeling helpless and at his mercy.

"I've never been able to admit this hatred toward my father before," Jane said. Uttering these words with some force seemed to lift a weight from her shoulders. "I'm glad you can feel this now," I said. It was clear that her hatred had frozen up inside and become turned against herself, and that owning it like this was an essential step in releasing herself from it.

Jane straightened up, and I asked her what was happening. She said, "I feel more solid, more contained." I invited her to describe this more. "There's an upright feeling, like I'm in my core. That feels powerful." It was clear that she was inhabiting herself more fully, and I encouraged her to stay with that sense of power in her body.

"There's a firmness in my belly and lower back. My mind is clear and the helplessness is gone."

"And how about Tom; right now, are you still hating him?"

"Tom?" she said, as though she were having a hard time remembering him. "I'm not even aware of Tom right now." When settled in herself, Tom's behavior wasn't such an issue.

Consciously experiencing her hatred instead of keeping it buried allowed Jane to unlock the power that was sealed up in it. And connecting with this power helped her start holding her ground when Tom wasn't there for her, instead of collapsing into resentful victimhood. This allowed her to speak her truth with him more directly, without the blame that usually triggered a fight.

At the end of all this work, Jane said, "I've been craving the experience of Tom being open to me, but now I realize I haven't been open to myself, especially in the places of hurt and fear and anger and hatred. It's amazing how when I do open to myself in these places, the urgent craving for Tom's love subsides. Because at least I have myself. And that's a lot."

It's important to recognize that acknowledging anger or hatred does not mean "Yes, it's right to be angry. I should feel hatred; I'm justified in feeling this way or in taking it out on someone." Instead it means "Yes, anger and hatred are there, stored up in my body and mind." And since they're there, "Yes, I can acknowledge them, give them room, and consciously experience them."

You may imagine that acknowledging feelings of anger or hatred will make you a more hateful or vengeful person. But in fact the reverse is true—as long as you consciously relate to the hatred as your own experience, rather than using it as a weapon for blaming and attacking the bad other. Denying or resisting your anger or hatred sets up an opposition within you that squelches your energy and diminishes your power. This keeps the aggression frozen inside you.

Yet when you can open to and stay present with the aggression, you free up the energy and power locked up in these feelings. The key is to give the energy of the anger or hatred plenty of room, and to ride the wave of that energy without focusing so much on the person with whom you're upset. Doing this lets you step out of the aggrieved victim role. In this way you find, paradoxically, that directly experiencing your hatred helps free you from hatred.

Hatred actually contains its own intelligence and truth. It is a signal that we are cut off from ourselves and the power of our being. This is what we most hate—feeling cut off from our power, our juice, our freedom, our ease, because of this bind we're in with another person. Through facing and directly experiencing the hatred, we can begin to decode the specific message that is hidden within it.

One day I asked the students in my group to explore their hatred in a conscious and deliberate way by first acknowledging the feeling in their body and then seeing what exactly they most hated in their relationships. These were a few of their responses: "I hate it when you turn away from me." "I hate it when there's no space for me in this relationship." "I hate it when you tell me how to be." "I hate it when you don't hear me." "I hate losing myself when I try to please you." "I hate the deadness I feel when I'm with you."

What my students most hated was how small and shut down they felt around another person. They were essentially saying, "I hate the way I shrink and lose touch with my own juice when I'm with you." And the crucial positive message hidden within their hatred was: "I want myself back. I don't want to let myself be so overwhelmed by how I feel with you that I lose myself." That is a statement of power.

Hatred is at bottom a cry for help, a cry for attention from a place in us that feels lost and disempowered. Recognizing hatred as a sign of disempowerment and helplessness allows us to make friends with it instead of regarding it as something evil. It becomes destructive only when we turn it into a weapon to use against ourselves or others.

Kind Understanding

What continues to fuel our grievance against other people is our aversion to the intense emotions—especially hurt, anger, and hatred—they trigger within us. Thus, to lay down our grievance and live at peace with the human race, or the person we live with, it's essential to make friends with these feelings. Learning to allow and open up space around the intense feelings and sensations in our body is a profound act of kindness that starts to melt down the ice of resentment that hardens the heart.

This inner kindness lets us take a further step in letting go of grievance: bringing understanding to the childhood circumstances in which our love-wound originally formed. A very special type of understanding is essential here—what I call *kind understanding* or *feeling-understanding* because it flows from the heart rather than from purely mental comprehension.

Why didn't your parents love you better? Why was their love so conditional or inconsistent? If you consider your parents not from the perspective of the aggrieved child but from that of an understanding adult, what you see are people who are hurt and wounded just like you. They also had their own share of burdens. They were struggling to make ends meet, keep their marriage together, and find themselves and their own way. All of these constraints and stresses made it hard for them to be there more fully for you.

In a tribal culture, others in the tribe—aunts, uncles, cousins, grandparents, neighbors—would have been there to take up the slack when your parents were not up to the task. But in our culture, the nuclear family is on its own. And the culture itself provides little wisdom, help, or guidance in raising children in a healthy way. So all the weight was on your parents to give you what you needed, and it was too much for them, given the other burdens they were carrying. No wonder their love seemed inconsistent and unreliable, and no wonder you came to distrust love.

On top of everything else, your parents had their own

legacy of not knowing they were loved, which made it hard for them to love themselves. When parents don't love themselves, they inevitably wind up using their children to shore up their shaky self-esteem. It requires a high degree of maturity to let loved ones be the unique, separate people that they are, with their own different needs, perspectives, and feelings. So, to the extent that your parents were not fully evolved themselves, they couldn't let you be who you were and simply love you for that.

This doesn't mean they were bad. Not knowing and loving oneself, not being confident in the beauty of one's own nature, is a general affliction that has been passed down through the generations. Your parents simply suffered from the same malady that afflicts everyone. Like everyone else, they were helpless in the face of their own conditioning.

Kind understanding is not a way to make excuses for your parents or condone the ways they were hurtful to you. Rather, recognizing that your parents' hurtful or negligent behavior arose out of their own wounding and lack of self-love is a step in liberating yourself. What does it feel like to see your parents' woundedness, without either justifying or condemning their behavior? They could not know or love you any better than they knew and loved themselves. If you have a little *feeling* of understanding for them and what they were up against, even the tiniest glimmer, this will help free you from the burden of grievance that you carry.

Not Taking It Personally

Just as your parents' imperfect love was not their fault, because they had no control over that, so too the lack of love that flowed your way is not *your* fault. In fact, it has nothing to do with you. For in truth, there are very few people in this world who have the capacity to truly see or know you as you are. No one else can see you or your beauty in a consistently accurate way. Your beauty is not a tangible thing but a subtle, inner quality that is often not visible from the outside.

There is no way to free yourself from the mood of unlove and the mood of grievance as long as you take it personally when others treat you badly. Taking it personally means imagining that it indicates something about who you are. As long as you take it personally when others don't see or appreciate you, you keep yourself imprisoned in the mind of the aggrieved child.

So when people treat you in negligent or hurtful ways, you could practice seeing their unkindness as a symptom of their inner tension and distress, arising out of their own inner disconnection. The man who tailgates you and insults you as he passes in his car is only acting out his own inner turmoil. He is in so much pain and stress that it clouds his consciousness. Unloading on you is a way of trying to reduce his tension and find some relief inside. If you take it personally, then you let his emotional turmoil enter your system and poison you. But if you don't take it personally, this frees you from the victim mind-state.

If your pain or anger comes up despite your best intentions not to take things personally, then don't take *that* personally either. Hurt and anger are just feelings, responses in your body arising out of your very human sensitivity to the events around you. You don't have to make them mean something bad about you. The more you work with hurt and anger in the ways described earlier, the more freedom you will have with these feelings. Then you can give them space, breathe into your belly, and open yourself to their energy as they move through you.

The Taoists have a famous teaching story about an empty boat that rams into your boat in the middle of a river. While you probably wouldn't be angry at an empty boat, you might well become enraged if someone were at its helm. The point of the story is that the parents who didn't see you, the other kids who teased you as a child, the driver who aggressively tailgated you yesterday—are in fact all empty, rudderless boats. They were compulsively driven to act as they did by their own unexamined wounds; therefore they did not know what they were doing and had little control over it.

Just as an empty boat that rams into us isn't targeting us, so too people who act unkindly are driven along by the unconscious force of their own wounding and pain. Until we realize this, we will remain prisoners of our grievance, our past, and our victim identity, all of which keep us from opening up to the more powerful currents of life and love that are always flowing through the present moment. Not taking it personally when someone hurts us is a profound practice of compassion, for ourselves first of all. It provides a breath of relief, allowing us to relax and let be in moments when our first impulse is to freeze up or lash out.

Loving-Kindness

Despite all the ways in which your parents failed to love you perfectly, you are only as healthy as you are today because of the ways they *did* care for you. Granted, their caring wasn't consistent. But if they hadn't shown you any kindness at all, you would not be well enough to be sitting here reading this book. You might be in an institution somewhere, or be a homeless person or a serial killer. So if you are relatively sane at all, this means that you most likely had what D. W. Winnicott calls "good enough" parents. If you find this hard to accept, you probably have more work to do unpacking and making friends with the hurt and anger you are carrying from the past.

In the final year of my mother's life, as it became apparent that she was on the decline, I was introduced to a powerful Tibetan contemplative practice that involves remembering the kindness of one's mother. The Tibetans use this as a first step toward developing compassion for all beings. Of course, this is easier for Tibetans because they cherish their mothers unequivocally. Like those of many American men, my feelings for my mother were clouded and ambivalent.

My mother's decline forced me to come to terms with an unpleasant reality that had marked my whole life: my grievance about her not being able to see or respect me as separate and different from her. All my life I had also felt burdened by her suffering, and by wanting to make her feel better so that I would feel better myself. And I had failed at that task, which left me filled with guilt and resentment. Again and again I had suffered the consequences of holding on to my grievance against her, the worst of which was my difficulty in letting myself be loved.

When I discovered this practice of remembering the kindness of my mother in the last year of her life, I felt immediately attracted to it. Though I had worked on my relationship with her in therapy with some success, this practice provided a simple, concrete method to reorient my whole attitude toward her. Letting myself remember and recognize all the countless ways she had shown me kindness helped me release my bad-other projections on her. I came to accept the fact that she could love me only in the ways that she was able to, given who she was and what she had been through.

Contemplating and appreciating her kindness also helped me open up my own in-channel so that I became more receptive to love in general. This helped me see the beauty of the practice of remembering others' kindness, for it is a way of learning to let yourself receive love, which is the basis for loving others. For this reason I am presenting a condensed version of this contemplative practice here. (People who still carry a heavy load of resentment toward their mother will probably not respond well to this exercise. If that is the case for you, I suggest not pushing it but working more on your hurt and anger first, or doing a similar exercise with someone else in your life who has been kind to you.)

Since it is easy to remember only the times when we think our mother harmed us and to forget her kindness or to take it for granted, we need to remember in detail how our mother has been kind from the very beginning of this life. In the beginning our mother was kind in offering us a place of birth. If she had wanted to evict us, she could have done so and we would not have been alive today to enjoy our present opportunities. When we were in our mother's womb, she protected us carefully, more carefully than she would guard a precious jewel. In every situation she thought of our safety. Even during the agony of childbirth, our welfare was foremost in her mind. When we were newly born, even though we looked more like a frog than a human being, our mother loved us dearly. Who cared for this scarcely human thing? It was our mother. She clothed it, cradled it, and fed it with her own milk. She removed the filth from its body without feeling any disgust.

While we were small, our mother was constantly watchful. Each day of our early childhood, our mother rescued us from many disasters. In the winter she would make sure that we were warm and had good clothing. She always selected the best things for us to eat, and she would rather have been sick herself than see us sick. As we grew older, our mother taught us to eat, drink, speak, sit, and walk. She sent us to school and encouraged us to do good things in life. When we became adolescent, we preferred to be with our friends and would completely forget our mother, and remember her only when we needed something from her. Yet our mother remained continuously concerned for us. Even though she may be old and weak and scarcely able to stand on her feet, she never forgets her children.

As you read this contemplation, you could see how it feels to consider these and other ways your mother may have cared for you. What kind of effect does that have on you? What happens to your grievance against your parents when you remember a few of these ways in which they did show you kindness? Assuming that you had "good enough" parents who were not total monsters, then recognizing their kindness can feel like letting sunshine into a dark dungeon.

Notice any tendency you may have to discount the kindness your parents or others have shown you. This is a barometer of your investment in grievance. There is a common tendency in relationships to focus on what is missing while underappreciating what is positive and available. We tend to take the good things for granted and fix our attention on what is wrong. This of course only leads to perpetual dissatisfaction and frustration, since no one else can give you everything you need or always love you in just the right way.

This tendency to focus on the negative—what's gone

wrong, what we're not getting—and to discount the positive—all that's going right, all that we *have* been given—is surely one of the most pernicious habits of the human mind. If we watch our mind at work, we can readily see how much more emphasis we put on the few things going wrong than on all the infinite things going right. As a chain saw starts up next door, our attention fixates on this disturbance, causing us to forget all about the lovely hours of silence that preceded and will also follow it.

There is a meal chant from the Zen Buddhist tradition that begins, "Seventy-two labors brought us this rice, we should know how it comes to us." Similarly, seventy-two labors have brought us everything we have, for we live in a network of human interconnectedness that supports our existence in every way. Even though life may not give us everything we want and contains all sorts of shocks and disappointments, everything that comes along can be a gift—by helping us wake up, develop new strength and resources, and become more loving human beings. In that sense, life is still generous and kind even when it manifests in shocking or ferocious ways.

At every moment we have the choice of either feeling gratitude for what has been given to us or indulging in grievance about what is missing. Grievance and gratitude are polar opposites. Grievance focuses on what is *not* there—the imperfections of relative love—and looks for someone to blame. Gratitude recognizes what *is* here—the simple beauty of human presence and contact—and responds to it with appreciation. When we reflect on how our life is possible only because it is held, surrounded, and nourished by a field of kindness, this gives rise to natural gratitude.

Of course, when we're in the grip of grievance, it is easy to discount the kindness that life and other people have shown us. If that is your tendency, see if you'd be willing to take a moment and explore how it feels to recognize just how much *has* been given to you. Or maybe you have a hard time acknowledging kindness shown to you because you feel undeserving, or guilty about not reciprocating. Yet despite these reactions, if you simply tune in to how your body feels when you receive kindness, you will notice the heart naturally expanding. No doubt this is why Rumi recommends that "whenever some kindness comes to you, turn that way, toward the source of kindness."

As the heart expands in gratefulness, we feel a natural desire to repay the kindness we have received, to give it back somehow. Gradually this develops into a basic wish that all beings be well, that the world live in peace, that everyone find true satisfaction. This is what Buddhists call loving-kindness. And out of loving-kindness arises compassion—not wanting anyone to suffer needlessly.

Notice the difference between how loving-kindness and grievance feel in your body. Grievance is tight, closed-in, and hard, while kindness is an expansive warmth, soft and open. This radiant warmth is your true nature finding its natural expression. Let it shine. This is natural forgiveness arising spontaneously—the beginning of the end of your investment in grievance.

CHAPTER FOUR

From Self-Hatred to Self-Love

There is no weapon for the realization of truth that is more powerful than this: to accept yourself.

—SWAMI PRAJNANPAD

You will never feel loved until you love yourself.

—ARNAUD DESJARDINS

IN THE END, we cannot hope to free ourselves from the stranglehold of grievance unless we relinquish the most destructive grievance of all—the one we hold against ourselves. Grievance always cuts two ways: Every grudge against the bad other for not treating me right or loving me properly is accompanied by a sense of bad self—a grievance against myself for not being good enough or worthy of that love. Bad other and bad self are two sides of the same coin.

Indeed, there would be no hatred of others without hatred of self. If we truly felt good about ourselves, we would have no interest in wasting precious life energy resenting or attacking anyone. The urge to blame others arises only out of feeling bad about ourselves, which originally developed out of not feeling truly seen or honored by other people. Self-hatred is the hidden underbelly of all the violence and nastiness in the world.

Self-hatred may seem like too strong a word to some. "I have a little self-doubt," you may say, "but I don't hate myself." Yet if you doubt, judge, or criticize yourself at all, this indicates some dislike or aversion toward yourself as you are. Or if you have a hard time spending time alone, undistracted by work, phone calls, television, computers, or other forms of busyness that pull your attention away from yourself, this also suggests that you may not like being with yourself all that much.

Unfortunately, the difficulty you have in loving and accepting yourself affects you even more profoundly than anyone else's lack of love. Whether you have a mild or an extreme case of self-hatred, it affects how you feel inside and how you experience your life every hour of every single day. It influences the thoughts you have, the choices you make, the actions you take, the lovers you select, and the relationships you create. In our culture, self-hatred is epidemic, infecting almost everyone to some degree, even those who manage to conceal it under a veneer of success or looking good.

Basic Goodness and Shame

It's not hard to see where the sense of bad self originated: not measuring up to other people's expectations. Maybe you were a shy, quiet child but your parents wanted their child to be more outgoing. Maybe your teachers expected verbal excellence but you were more interested in art, music, and dance. Or maybe your full-bodied exuberance scared off the boys, who were looking for someone who didn't threaten them.

Nonetheless, the bad self is only a thought in the mind, nothing more. It develops through taking it personally when others don't see or appreciate us: "What's wrong with me, that no one really sees or appreciates who I am?" This pattern became established when we were young: "Why are my parents so angry or neglectful toward me? There must be something wrong with me, that's why." That is the only way a child can understand neglect or abuse. As a result, we wind up disliking who we are: "If only I were different, then I would be loved, and everything would be okay."

In this way shame—the feeling that the self we are is no good—takes up residence in the body and mind. Shame is undoubtedly the most painful of all feelings. That's because it denies the vital truth—that our basic nature is intrinsically beautiful and good.

This notion of basic goodness is not some New Age Pollyanna creed. Mystics and sages East and West, from Plato to Lao-tzu and the Buddha, have directly experienced the essence of human nature as a natural purity of heart, from which all positive qualities flow: love, caring, courage, humor, wisdom, devotion, strength. As an inherent quality of our nature, this good-heartedness is more fundamental than any notion we have about being good or bad based on our behavior or acceptance by others. An unshakable sense of our intrinsic value can only develop through coming to experience and know the essential purity and nobility at our core.

By causing us to doubt our basic goodness and thus negating the truth of who we are, shame is paralyzing. It causes our nervous system to freeze up and shut down. And since this sense of bad self feels so painful, we try our best to ward it off. So, like the bad other, the bad-self image also falls into unconsciousness, affecting us in automatic ways over which we have little control.

One way the bad-self image comes back to haunt us is in a stream of negative self-talk—what I call the "inner critic." The critic is the voice that tells us that nothing we do is ever good enough. It dwells below the threshold of consciousness, waiting for the slightest justification to come out and go on the attack. A simple way to observe the critic in action is by looking at yourself in the mirror. How do you react to that face staring back at you? If you see signs of aging, how do you regard yourself? Do you feel kindness and unconditional acceptance toward the face in the mirror? Or do you judge yourself harshly for not measuring up to some standard?

If you could peer into the thoughts in most people's minds, you would find most of them revolving around a single preoccupation: "Am I okay or not?" This is what fuels the fixation "she [he] loves me, she [he] loves me not." If she loves me, then maybe I am a good self after all—someone successful, attractive, likable, strong—and I can feel good about myself. But if she loves me not, then I am thrown into the hell of seeing myself as the bad self—someone inadequate, unattractive, unsuccessful, unlovable, or weak. And then I hate and reject myself.

Thus an inner trial is going on in the background of the mind as we continually marshal evidence for one side or the other: "People responded well to me today, so I feel good about myself." "People didn't respond well to me today, so maybe I'm not okay after all."

Why do we allow the critic to live on within us, with all its painful consequences? To the extent that we don't know we're intrinsically lovable, we don't believe love will ever just come to us on its own. We believe instead that we have to *do* something to make ourselves acceptable. So to push ourselves to try harder to be good, to whip ourselves into shape, we hire an in-house critic to keep tabs on how we're doing. If we can prove that we are worthy, then maybe we will be loved.

Unfortunately, this inner trial—"Am I good enough yet? No, I could still do a lot better"—is endless and fruitless. Trying to be good can never result in a secure sense of inner value because this very effort presupposes that we are *not* good enough and thus only reinforces our self-hatred. This sense of unworthiness also makes it hard to let love in, even when it is available. Not loving ourselves makes it hard to let others really love us. This frustrates those who are there for us, causing them to withdraw or leave. And then we use that as further evidence that there's something wrong with us. In this way, the bad-self story becomes a self-fulfilling prophecy.

Just as it was frustrating having to be a good boy or a good girl to win our parents' acceptance—because then we never felt loved just as we were—so it is with trying to win the critic's approval by proving we are worthy. The self-acceptance that can heal self-hatred and shame will never arrive through winning a favorable verdict in the inner trial. It can arise only out of recognizing and appreciating the being we actually are, in our unconditional goodness and beauty, where we know ourselves as something much more vast and real than any notion we have about good self or bad self.

Acting Out the Wound

Self-hatred also fuels grievance and violence against others in a fairly predictable way: We try to transfer our own bad feelings onto other people as a way to feel less bad ourselves. While this takes an especially grisly form in public displays of scapegoating and warfare, the same dynamic operates to some extent in most human relationships.

Discharging aggression on others is a classic way of trying to alleviate the shame or self-hatred that comes up in relationships. It could be something as simple as a wife making a sharp remark about her husband driving too fast. If he hears this as blame, it may trigger his inner critic. Then, to defend against feeling like the bad self, he makes her into the bad other instead. He counterattacks, blaming her for nagging him. Now she feels like the bad self, and to ward off her own critic she in turn tries to make him the bad other: "Why are you always so defensive?" And he retorts: "Why are you always so critical?"

This is what couples do all the time—tossing the sense of badness back and forth like a hot potato. No wonder marriage partners become so invested in being right, even if it destroys their relationship. Being right is a way of trying to deflect the critic's attack, with its crippling self-hatred and shame. It is always very sad to see two people who love each other going at each other this way.

One of the shortcomings of conventional religion is that it often speaks in the voice of the critic, blaming people for their sins and unworthiness. Instead of castigating people for their faults, it would be far more compassionate and skillful to help people see how the so-called deadly sins are all symptoms of not knowing that they're loved.

Greed, for example, grows out of an inner sense of hunger, "I don't have enough," under which lies an even deeper sense of "I'm not enough." Yet what is this inner poverty that we try to relieve through consuming and possessing, if not the emptiness of feeling cut off from love? Fire-and-brimstone moralists would have us believe that greed is proof of our sinfulness. But perhaps greed is only as compelling as it is because it promises to relieve our deprivation, yet without ever delivering the real goods, thus leaving us ever more prey to our hunger, which only the food of love can truly satisfy.

Likewise, jealousy only arises out of lack of confidence in being loved: Somehow life is loving others more than me. Similarly, self-centeredness, arrogance, and pride are attempts to make ourselves important or special, as a way to make up for a lack of genuine self-love. Egocentricity is a way of trying to make the world revolve around "me," to compensate for an underlying fear that I don't really matter much at all. If we felt loved, it would of course never occur to us that we didn't matter.

And what drives people to seek power over others? Why would anyone want to spend this short, precious life pursuing the chimera of empire building or world domination? What's the thrill in that? Power over others is a way of trying to prove that I am somebody, to force others to look up to me: "I'll get you to respect me one way or another, even if it means torturing or killing you." If I can show you I'm really somebody—the chief honcho, the dictator, the world conqueror, the filthy-rich magnate—then you will have to look up to me, and then maybe I can feel good about myself. But if I felt held in love, there would be no reason to try to set myself above you.

Behind all the evils of the world is the pain of a wounded, disconnected heart. We behave badly because we hurt inside. And we hurt because our basic nature is wide open and tender to begin with. Thus all the ugliness in the world can be traced back to turning away from our raw and beautiful heart.

When we recognize this—that the sins of the world are but symptoms of the universal wound—we can understand the words of the French spiritual teacher Arnaud Desjardins when he writes: "There are no bad people (including Stalin and Hitler, who were responsible for the deaths of millions)—only badly loved people." Here the root of all evil is laid bare: *There are no bad people, only badly loved people.* If Stalin, Hitler, or Osama bin Laden experienced themselves as loved and lovable, what motivation would they have to kill? Feeling love circulating through you makes you want to celebrate and nurture life, not destroy it.

Of course, dictators like Stalin or Hitler don't realize what is driving them, because they have buried the pain of their wounding underneath many layers of grievance, hardening, and self-aggrandizement. No doubt it would take many years of psychotherapy to unpack the ways that they are bruised, badly loved souls in need of tender, loving care. "If Stalin had been truly loved," as Desjardins points out, "he would not have killed twenty million people."

The same holds true for humanity as a whole. Imagine for a moment humanity as an individual. If this fellow called Humanity knew himself as truly lovable, as a wondrous being whose essential nature was to bring luminous love and wisdom into this world, would he need to continue blindly destroying the planet while indulging in senseless violence and vengeance? As long as Humanity fails to recognize his basic goodness, he can only act in pathological, self-destructive ways. And when he stops for a moment to look at all the havoc he's caused, he can only conclude that he is a miserable creature indeed. Meanwhile, the news media serve as a mirror in which Humanity looks at himself each day, reflecting back to him lurid, degraded images of what he is. How can poor old Humanity come to love himself when, continually seeing through this glass darkly, he witnesses only his own pettiness, depravity, and ugliness?

Humanity as a whole is still a child in need of healing, in need of knowing that it is beautiful in its very nature. In traditional cultures, art, mythology, religion, and ritual helped humanity remember its divine essence. But today, lacking tradition, each of us must heal the heart and wake up to our inner beauty on our own, for the sake of humanity.

The good news is that all the things we are most ashamed of, all of our so-called deadly sins, are only paper tigers. Look behind the tiger's snarl and you find a sad, lonely, desperate child who feels disconnected from love. This brings all the horrors of the world down to size. The heart closing itself off to love is the origin of all bad karma, sending out shock waves that reverberate around the world.

Letting Yourself Have Your Experience

Since we can never gain assurance that we are lovable through trying to prove our worth or hide our flaws, what we need instead is a way to discover our core nature as intrinsically beautiful, already, just as it is. This is what can free us from the whole bad-self/bad-other runaround.

The journey from self-hatred to self-love involves learning to meet, accept, and open to the being that you are. This begins with *letting yourself have your experience*. Genuine self-love is not possible as long as you are resisting, avoiding, judging, or trying to manipulate and control what you experience. Whenever you judge what you're experiencing—"I shouldn't be having this experience. It's not good enough. I should be having some better experience than this one"—you're not letting yourself be as you are. This aggravates the core wound of "I'm not acceptable as I am." And it sets you at odds with yourself, creating inner division and turmoil. The way to free yourself from shame and self-blame is through developing a more friendly relationship with your experience, no matter what experience you're having.

Letting ourselves have our experience can be quite challenging, since nobody ever taught us how to relate honestly and directly to what we were feeling. Instead, the conventional wisdom in our culture is: If you're depressed or anxious, take a pill, go work out at the gym, or turn on the television—because the only solution to bad feelings is to get away from them.

Often when I try to help people open to their experience, they say something like: "I've felt this sadness all my life. What good is it to sit here and keep feeling it? I've already had enough of this!" While this is understandable, the voice that says, "If I feel my sadness, it will just pull me down into a bottomless black hole," comes from the helpless child who has never learned to handle his or her experience. For the child, it was true: Our sadness was bigger than we were because we didn't have the knowledge or capacity to process intense feelings. So our only choice was to shut down our nervous system in the face of our pain. The problem is that we still try to run away from our feelings, even though as an adult we now have the capacity to do something different.

So yes, we have carried our pain within us all of our lives. Yes, we have felt weighed down by it, and been at its mercy. Since the pain was bigger than we were as children, and we were helpless in the face of it, shutting down was the only way we could deal with it. So it's understandable that we see no benefit in opening ourselves to such feelings. And it's true: Passively becoming submerged or carried away by feelings *is* useless and futile. It is *unconscious suffering.*

This is not what I mean by letting yourself have your experience. I mean the very opposite: actively meeting, engaging, and opening to what you're feeling. Consciously touching a feeling—"yes, this is the feeling that's there"— starts to free you from its grip. If you can open to your fear or pain and put your attention on experiencing the openness itself, eventually you may discover something marvelous: Your openness is more powerful than the feelings you're opening to. Openness to fear is much bigger and stronger than the fear itself. This discovery puts you in touch with your capacity for strength, kindness, stability, and understanding in the face of whatever you are going through. This is *conscious suffering.*

If there is one thing I have learned in thirty years as a psychotherapist, it is this: If you can let your experience happen, it will release its knots and unfold, leading to a deeper, more grounded experience of yourself. No matter how painful or scary your feelings appear to be, your willingness to engage with them draws forth your essential strength, leading in a more life-positive direction. My work, both with other people and with myself, has thoroughly convinced me of this truth, which has become the bedrock of my therapeutic practice.

Just as the depth and stillness of the ocean lie hidden beneath the stormy waves on its surface, so the power of your essential nature lies concealed behind all of your turbulent feelings. Struggling against your feelings only keeps you tossing around on the stormy surface of yourself, disconnected from your larger being. Tossing in the waves keeps you from going beneath them and accessing the power, warmth, and openness of the heart.

Letting yourself have your experience, by contrast, allows you to ride or surf the waves instead of being carried away by them. In moments of allowing and opening to your experience, *you are*—you are there for yourself. You are saying yes to yourself as you are, as you are feeling right now. This is a profound act of self-love.

How then to start letting yourself have your experience? How to make friends with your feelings, just as they are in this moment, no matter how difficult they may be? The key is always to start right here where you are, wherever that is.

For instance, if you're confused or disturbed right now by what I'm suggesting, you could start by simply acknowledging the confusion or disturbance without judging it as something bad or trying to get rid of it. Or, if you would be willing to tune in to the place of unlove within you, you could see how it feels in your body. Simply *acknowledge* the sensations in your body and touch them with your awareness, while staying aware of your breathing: "Yes, this is what's here." When you give up struggling to ward off your experience, you start to relax.

Next, *allow* the feeling to be there, giving it plenty of space. Allowing doesn't mean wallowing in the feeling or acting it out, but rather opening up space around the sensations in your body. This is like giving the feeling some breathing room so it is not confined or constricted. Experience the space around the feeling and notice how the space lets the feeling be there, just as it is, without tension or resistance. Let yourself rest in that space. As you do this, you will find that you are holding the feeling in a much softer way. You have become the larger awareness in which your woundedness is held. Then there is nothing to fight against, and the body starts to settle down.

Once you settle, you could also go a little further and see if you can *open* yourself to feeling the unlove directly, not maintaining any barrier against it. Be kind and understanding toward it, as you would toward your child or your dearest friend if he or she were hurting. A further, more advanced step is to *enter* with your awareness right into the center of the feeling, softening into it, so that you are at one with the feeling, not separate from it in the least.

When you can enter and relax into a feeling, it no longer remains something *other* that can torment or overwhelm you. When you can be present in the center of a feeling, you discover its nature as fluid energy. If the wound of unlove is undigested pain from childhood, then letting yourself experience it with unconditional presence is a way of digesting that old pain. Then it no longer remains something solid and frozen that clogs your system. This is a simple and direct way of starting to heal your woundedness, the fearful shutdown you became stuck in as a child.

Being present with yourself like this is an act of love that unlocks the door to your deepest resources. There is a simple principle operating here: When you show up for your experience, your being shows up for you. And when the larger being that you truly are reveals itself, you have an experience of coming home to yourself. Settling into yourself gives you access to native resources—strength, acceptance, peace, compassion—that help you meet and relate to whatever you're going through.

Coming home to yourself and your resources, you discover what is more true than any self-judgment: that you are just fine as you are, in your basic nature. You taste the basic goodness inherent within you, which has a clear, refreshing taste like pure water. Discovering this helps you appreciate your life, even with all its difficulties. Letting yourself have your experience is the gateway to self-acceptance and self-love.

Letting Yourself Be the Being That You Are

Yet what exactly is self-love? In my experience, it is something much more subtle and profound than the pep talk pick-me-ups promoted by self-help gurus who proclaim, "Believe in yourself, you're fantastic, and doggone it, people like you!"

Self-love is something much more sacred and mysterious than that. It is an inner glow or atmosphere of warmth that gradually begins to infuse you as you learn to say yes to yourself as you are, in this very moment. This is an essential basis for spiritual growth, as Swami Prajnanpad recognized when he said, "The most important thing of all is to love yourself."

The most loving thing you can do for yourself is to let yourself be. Be what? The being that you are, of course. This is the definition of self-love that I propose: *letting yourself be the being that you are.*

Are you aware of this being that you are, this being that wants to live in you, through you, as you? If you're truthful, you may admit you barely know this deeper dimension of yourself at all. This being that you are can only be found right here in the core of your living experience in this very moment. Everything else is but a memory or mental projection.

The being that you are is not something you can wrap your mind around. It is beyond anything you can think. Though you may bristle when others impose their ideas on you or put you in some narrow conceptual box, you probably don't notice how much you do this to yourself. Who you were yesterday, last year, or in childhood, adolescence, young adulthood—none of these is who you are; they are only memories. Holding in mind a picture or concept of who you are puts you in a soul-cage that keeps you from living freely and expansively.

Of course, if you hold beliefs that you are bad, unworthy, or deficient, then it can be a helpful first step to think of yourself as good, to see yourself in a more positive or compassionate light. For many people, this kind of positive affirmation can be a useful step on the way toward genuine self-love. But this is still a conceptual exercise that splits us in two: a separate I, the subject, appreciating a separate me, the object of that love. For self-love to truly come alive, it has to be more than just a concept, a belief, or self-talk. It has to involve a new way of inhabiting myself, of feeling and celebrating the living presence that I am, rather than just maintaining some favorable self-image.

Self-love involves a yes to myself in whatever I am going through, instead of holding on to some concept of what or how I should be. Any idea I have about who I am or who I should be is never accurate, for it always falls short of the living presence that I am, as this unfolds freshly in each new moment. Who I am is not a fixed entity but a dynamic stream of experiencing that is alive in every moment—when I let myself happen.

You can have a taste of what I'm describing here by simply dropping any notion you have of yourself right now. What happens when you let yourself just be here, right in this moment, without relying on any of the familiar images and beliefs stored on the "hard disk" of memory to tell you who you are? At first there may be a sense of disorientation. If you can simply relax into that for a moment, without recoiling in fear, there may be a moment of sensing yourself freshly as a living presence, a mysterious, unfathomable being who is open and awake and ready to respond to the changing currents of each moment.

Let yourself be that being, if only at first for a moment here and there. This will help you settle down and connect with yourself, providing a fresh and immediate taste of your inherent dignity and value. Fresh moments like these make it possible to be happy just to be alive, just to be the being that you are. The more you taste this inner connectedness, the more it gives rise to an inner glow, which is the direct, immediate experience of self-love.

Saying Yes to Yourself

Saying yes to yourself also means accepting the messy, imperfect human that you are. "It was easy to love God in all that was beautiful," wrote Saint Francis. Yet he recognized that for love to be the real thing, it must encompass everything, including all of life's darkness and pain. So he went on to say, "The lessons of deeper knowledge, though, instructed me to embrace God in all things."

How to embrace God in all things within yourself? Not just in the beauty but also in the heart of the beast? As the German spiritual teacher Rudi (Swami Rudrananda) wrote:

The only thing that can create a oneness inside you is the ability to see more of yourself as you work every day to open deeper, and to say, "Fine, I'm short-tempered," or "I'm aggressive," or "I love to make money," or "I have no feeling for anyone else." Once you recognize that you are all of these things . . . you will finally be able to take a breath and allow these things to open. . . . Your ego and prejudices and limitations are your raw material. Out of the raw material you break down, you grow and absorb the energy. If you process and refine it all, you can open consciously. Otherwise you will never come to anything that represents yourself.

In a similar vein, a participant in one of my workshops told a story about an experience she had of discovering self-love in a most unexpected way: "I had been going through a period of intense stress about certain events in my life that triggered a great deal of pain and self-hatred. One day I was finally forced to admit, 'The truth is, right now I am a completely fucked-up human being and cannot be anything other than that.' I had never acknowledged anything quite like that before. My story has always been about being 'together'— whether that meant being the best student in the class or the most spiritually realized person. So stripping away all the layers of regret or apology about being so messed up was quite profound for me. And as I let myself be irredeemably fucked up and, at least for the moment, incapable of being anything other than that, doorways began opening for me. They kept opening and opening. And, having failed to live up to all of my concepts about what self-love was supposed to be based on, I had an experience of loving myself that was totally nonconceptual. I felt rooted in myself in a direct, immediate way because all my ideas about what it meant to be rooted in my-self had completely dissolved. I had come home to myself in a way I could not have imagined before."

Usually we cannot bear to face the raw, messy, wounded parts of ourselves because we fear that the critic will prose-cute us for them, using them as evidence to frame us as the beastly bad self. Letting ourselves be the being that we are, however, means giving up trying to be a good self, because we recognize that all our ideas of ourselves as good self or bad self are merely concepts in the mind.

You can develop a simple practice of saying yes to yourself each day. Stop for a moment, pay attention to whatever's going on inside you, and then acknowledge it in a neutral way: "Yes, this is what's here." "Yes, I'm nervous," lightly meeting or touching the nervousness with your awareness. *Don't reject anything you are experiencing.* Meet it instead in a brief moment of nonjudgmental awareness—touching it and letting it be. This is a simple way of saying yes to yourself, a shorthand form of unconditional love and presence that you can practice at any moment, wherever you are, whatever you are doing.

"Yes, there's worry." Touch that and let be, lightly making contact with the sense of worry in your body. "Yes, I'm acting in a stingy way," and notice how it affects you to be aware of that, without judgment or manipulation. *Yes* here does not mean, "I like it," "I approve of it," "I think it's good," or "I'm glad it's like this." It simply means, "Yes, this is what's here right now. I can meet this because it's what is happening. And I can stay open to myself even though this is coming up." When you can offer that kind of yes to yourself, it silences the critic and puts a stop to the inner trial.

If you have a hard time saying yes to something, you can also say yes to that: "Yes, I am struggling with this; I'm having a hard time letting it be." "Yes, I'm not accepting this right now; there's a refusal in me." Notice and feel the resistance or refusal and let it be, with awareness. Don't just observe it, but feel it and give it room to have its energetic play, while remaining aware of it nonjudgmentally. If you judge, then be aware of that, and again: "Yes, there is judgment." Let the judgment simply be there in awareness, without judging the judgment. "Yes, I am here for myself even though self-judgment is arising." See if you can be an interested, neutral witness of what happens in your mind and emotions, extending warmth and openness to whatever is there, in the spirit of "Yes, yes, this is what's here."

Don't let this be a conceptual exercise. You don't have to verbalize the "yes," though that can often be helpful. What's most important is to touch what's there for a moment, let it be, and experience yourself there with it, in openness, allowing yourself to be as you are, even though you may not like what you are feeling. "Yes, I can be here with myself even though anxiety is arising . . . even though self-doubt is present . . . even though loneliness is here."

As you open briefly to whatever state you're in, directly experience the openness that can see and let be. Notice that this openness is much larger than any of the states you go through. *Be* this openness, which can hold your experience in a kind and gentle way. This puts you in touch with the larger being that you are, who is not trapped in any of these states of mind.

Above all, don't identify with any of the states you pass through, don't make them mean something about you. ("I'm afraid. . . . That means I'm a fearful person. . . . I've always been that way. . . . It's just the way I am.") When you acknowledge, "I'm afraid," this doesn't mean that fear is who you are. Instead, it's a shorthand way of saying, "I'm aware of fear arising in my body and mind." The "I" that can recognize the fear is not itself afraid. It is the larger being that you are, the awareness that can see and hold whatever's there in you— all the qualities, all the feelings, all the tight spots, all the conditioned patterns.

But if you do find yourself stuck in identifying, acknowledge that in a kindly way as well: "Okay, now I'm taking this personally," and see what it's like to recognize that without making it wrong.

Saying yes to whatever is there in you is a way of calling forth the larger awareness that can hold all of your experience in a space of warmth and openness. Over time you will see how this lightens and frees you up. As Swami Prajnanpad sums up this core principle of self-love: "Say yes to everything. Reject nothing, least of all something in yourself."

Kind Understanding for Yourself

Learning to accept your human experience as just what it is, imperfect as it is, brings kind understanding into the places where you've held grievances against yourself. For instance, what do you typically give yourself a hard time about or blame yourself for? Try to articulate this in a single sentence. If you have a number of different grievances—"I'm lazy," "I eat too much," "I don't try hard enough," "I'm selfish," "I've hurt people," or "I'm cowardly"—choose one that cuts deep.

Grievances against yourself usually contain two elements: a certain clear discernment mixed together with a harsh-critic judgment. For example, you recognize that you are selfish, but then you judge that as a sign that something's wrong with you. Take a moment to tease these two elements apart, separating the discernment from the blame. See if you can set the blame aside. Then put what you discern about yourself in front of you and look at it as though you were an all-wise, all-loving, all-understanding parent, friend, or teacher.

For instance, if your grievance is "I'm selfish," put aside any self-blame and see what the all-wise part of you understands about this. Maybe you see that it arises out of your childhood insecurity about being cared for—which caused you to try to meet your needs in a grasping, inconsiderate way. Addressing the selfish place directly, your understanding might say something like: "Your experience as a child was that if you didn't look out for yourself, no one else would. No wonder you feel compelled to grab hold of whatever you can. It's a way of trying to feel secure."

A woman in one of my groups judged herself for not speaking up for what she wanted. Her kind understanding was: "You were never allowed to have your own ideas and feelings as a child. Whenever you expressed what you felt or believed, you were told to be quiet. No one ever supported you in having your own voice. No wonder you're afraid to speak up." When I asked this woman how she felt after saying this, she said, "When I first felt the self-judgment, my chest tightened up. But now I feel compassion for myself, and warmth is streaming into my limbs."

This woman had already known that she didn't speak up because no one had ever encouraged her as a child, so that was nothing new. What was new in this experience was *feeling* understanding toward herself about this, which allowed her to open her heart to herself.

So in practicing kind understanding, it's important to feel how the understanding affects you. When you have genuine understanding for yourself, it is like a warm embrace that releases soothing energy in the body. Let yourself feel what that's like. Though you often try to get others to understand you, the understanding that heals the most is your own. As the warmth of understanding starts to flow, it washes away your grievance against yourself, allowing self-love to take its place.

Appreciating What Is Yours

A further stage in the growth of self-love is being able to appreciate what is uniquely yours to offer. Each of us has a special contribution to make to this world, especially when we emerge as the being that we are. The uniqueness of the individual, according to Martin Buber, is the bearing of a special gift. What you bring into this world through your particular quality of being—no one else can manifest this in the same way that you can. In Buber's words:

> Every person born into this world represents something new, something that never existed before, something original and unique. It is the duty of every person . . . to know and consider . . . that there has never been anyone like him in the world, for if there had been someone like him, there would have been no need for him to be in the world. Every single person is a new thing in the world and is called upon to fulfill his particularity in this world. Every person's foremost task is the actualization of his unique, unprecedented and never-recurring potentialities, and not the repetition of something that another, be it even the greatest, has already achieved.

> The same idea was expressed by Rabbi Zusya when he said a short while before his death: "In the world to come I shall not be asked, 'Why where you not Moses?' I shall be asked, 'Why were you not Zusya?'"

What does it mean to be yourself in this sense, to "be Zusya"? It means saying yes to the being that you are. Only then is it possible for the unique offering that your existence represents to manifest fully.

The habit of comparing ourselves to others or trying to be like them is one of the greatest obstacles to self-love. This preoccupation with whether we are like others, or better or worse than them, is a way of dishonoring ourselves. As a writer, for instance, I have often felt envious of colleagues who write books quickly. One friend has written books in three to six months that have become major best sellers. My books, by contrast, have always taken a few years to complete and have not as yet flown up the best-seller charts the way his have.

I can fall into wishing I could write quickly and easily like my friend. Yet to be honest with myself, I also have to recognize that his books are not the kind that are mine to write. Letting myself be the being that I am means appreciating the particular journey I am on and the way my writing reflects that, instead of trying to write like someone else. After all, no one else can speak with my voice. As long as I can't appreciate what is mine to offer, I set up roadblocks to what wants to come through me.

Similarly, each of us has some gift that is uniquely ours. One person might be a special kind of mother, another might be a powerful communicator, another might be a sensitive listener. Someone else might be fiercely dedicated to truth, while another might have the capacity to inspire people to do their best. The beauty in these gifts can shine forth only when we appreciate what wants to come through us, without trying to live up to some preconceived standard in our mind.

Moreover, even this description of people's gifts falls short of the mark, for the most special gift that you have to offer is the living quality of your presence, the indescribable spark that makes you *you*. Each soul has its own multifaceted, jewel-like character, its own "suchness." Even though no one can exactly pin down this "special something," it's what people love when they love you. Suchness means *just so*. You are just so in your way; I am just so in mine. We are all just what we are, and cannot be other than what we are in the end. This is cause for celebration.

Loving yourself as you are may sound like egoism to some. But in truth, it provides the most powerful basis of all for loving others. For, letting yourself be the being that you are helps you recognize the importance of letting others be who they are as well. One of the most loving things you can do is to let others be different from you and to free them from your demands and expectations. When you kindly understand that others have their own laws and must follow their own way, just as you do, the need to control them or make yourself more important than them starts to fall away.

The elements of self-love explored in this chapter—loosening up your self-concepts, letting yourself have your experience, letting yourself be the being that you are, saying yes to yourself, understanding your weaknesses with kindness, and appreciating the unique gift your life has to offer—are all ways of opening your heart to yourself. And this is the indispensable key that will unlock the door through which absolute, perfect love can enter and take up residence within you.

CHAPTER FIVE

Holy Longing

You see, I want a lot.
Perhaps I want everything.

—RAINER MARIA RILKE

The intensity of the longing
Does all the work.

—KABIR

SAYING YES TO OURSELVES, letting ourselves be as we are, opening our heart to ourselves—all of this serves to kindle the inner glow of self-love, bringing healing to our core wound. One more element still needs to fall into place, however, if we are to free ourselves from the mood of unlove: We must be able to let love all the way into us.

Yet how is this possible if our capacity to open to love has been damaged by the devastations of hurt, distrust, and fear? Fortunately, there is a simple and obvious place to start—from our very desire and need for love itself.

This can be challenging, since we may also have a troubled relationship with our wanting. We may have learned at an early age that our need for love subjected us to danger. Children of parents who are emotionally distant must often shut down or deny their longing for love because it is too painful to keep subjecting themselves to so much frustration and unfulfilled desire. And children of parents who are overly intrusive or controlling often have to cut off their need for connection so that they can more easily forge a separate life of their own.

As a result of these early conflicts, most of us grow up judging or denying our need for love. We may become ashamed or afraid of our desire, which we associate with intense vulnerability, sorrow, or deprivation. A further obstacle for some is religious teaching they have absorbed that condemns desire as a sign of their crude, animal nature, dragging them down into the mud. So even though our wish for love is undeniable, it often feels too threatening to let ourselves fully acknowledge it. Even though we can't help wanting, we don't want to want.

In this way, our relation to desire becomes troubled and we experience it as something that diminishes us. And since we are not on good terms with our wanting, we have a hard time expressing it cleanly and unapologetically. We often pretend to ourselves or others that we don't really want what we want.

We cannot receive love, however, if we are not open to the raw and tender experience of wanting it. Suppressing or denying desire shuts down our openness to receiving nourishment, and thus only intensifies our hunger.

Perhaps if we could make friends with it, we might find that our wanting itself is holy. We want love, after all, because we intuitively know that it can free us from the prison of the isolated self, allowing us to feel connected and at one with all of life. What is so bad about wanting that?

Making Desire Transparent

In working with couples, I commonly find that one or both partners have trouble stating their desire clearly, or even recognizing what it is they want. When I invite them to express their wanting directly, what often comes out instead is complaint, demand, evasiveness, or speechmaking. They can easily say what their partner is doing wrong or failing to give them. But when it comes to expressing their actual desire, there is uncertainty or hesitation.

Why is it so much easier to complain, collapse, make demands, or attack than to openly express what we want? The answer is simple: Complaint and demand provide a defensive shield to hide behind, while desire makes us feel exposed. Letting others see how much we want their love means letting down our defenses and baring our soul. This is even more difficult if our sentry is constantly on guard against the bad other who isn't there for us. Thus it's not surprising that exposing our desire for love is not something we want to do. It's much easier to play it safe by focusing on how others don't give us what we want.

Julie and Rick were on the verge of divorce after staying together through twelve years of marriage and the birth of three children. Rick was already half-gone, having initiated a period of trial separation. His basic complaint was that Julie's heart was not open to him, while her complaint was that he was not committed to the relationship.

Julie acknowledged that she had problems opening her heart to anyone, out of fear of abandonment dating back to childhood. So it was much easier for her to complain about Rick's lack of commitment than it was for her to show Rick how much she wanted him to accept her, especially now that he already had one foot out the door. When I asked her what she most wanted in the relationship, her first statement was:

"I want to know that Rick is committed."

"Can you say what that means to you? What is the experience you're wanting to have with him?"

"I don't trust that he is really there for me."

Here again she was complaining. I invited her to turn that into a statement of what she wanted: "So you want to know that he can really be there for you."

"Yes."

"Can you tell him that directly?"

Turning to Rick, Julie sat there for a while, hesitant and anxious. Finally she said, "I want you to be committed." But this sounded like a command or demand, as though she were building a case, rather than transparently disclosing what was true for her.

"Are you wanting that right now?" I asked her.

"Uh, yes," she said hesitantly.

"Do you? Check it out inside, and see if that's true right now in this moment."

"Yes, I'd like that."

"Can you let him see that?"

She again turned to Rick and paused. Then she said, quickly and simply, "I really want to feel that you're here with me." This time as she said it, her words had more resonance. She was actually feeling her desire as she spoke, right on the spot. It was no longer a demand but a transparent wish that invited Rick in. He immediately sat up and took notice. He was obviously touched.

I asked him how it was for him to have Julie express that. He said, "It's great. I can really respond to that." Turning to Julie, he said, "That makes me feel that I *do* want to be here with you." Since being able to see into Julie's heart was the very thing he wanted, her transparency invited and inspired him to show up more fully as well.

Julie was a bit confused. She didn't understand what had just happened, why he suddenly responded to her so warmly, when he hadn't so many times before. I said to her, "It's like this: When you said you wanted to feel him here with you, *you* were really here, *you* were showing up. And that's what he most wants: to feel that your heart is open and transparent, not hidden behind your complaint." In letting her partner see how much she wanted him to show up, she was showing up herself. In asking him to be there, with her heart exposed, *she* was there, nakedly. This allowed him to feel connected with her, which was what *he* most wanted.

It often takes some work for two partners to acknowledge and reveal their deep wish to feel loved. But when either of them can do this, without blame or demand, there is an instant sense of relief—on both sides. It's a tremendous relief to get down to the simple truth and express it openly: "I really want to feel your love."

The partner who receives this message can also relax, because he or she no longer has to ward off the other's complaint or demand. But there is an even deeper relief for the listening partner: When others reveal their desire in a transparent, undefended way, they are letting you see them, which provides an entry point that allows contact to happen. Moments of naked truth-telling unveil your partner's beauty, allowing you to suddenly reconnect with why you fell in love with this person in the first place.

This kind of electric moment also happens frequently when I work with couples in front of a group. When one partner simply reveals what he or she most wants, all the people in the room find themselves instantly riveted to that person. Everyone feels natural empathy without even having to think about it.

It's vital to understand the principle at work here, for it is what will allow us to receive not just human love, but also absolute love from the source. The essential point is to become transparent—by letting our deep longing for love and connectedness be exposed. This makes us porous, opening up the channel through which love can enter.

The Spectrum of Desire

Of course, when we experience the full force of our desire for love, this can also make us feel unsettled, overwhelmed, swept away. But it's important to realize that it's not desire itself that is so overpowering. Desire becomes overwhelming only when it attaches or glues itself to an object that we imagine we *must have* in order to feel okay. It's this fixation on an external object, this obsession, that becomes disempowering and enslaving.

In its essential nature, desire is radiant heat. It is an upsurge of bodily excitement, of raw life force that wants to reach out, make contact, and connect with the life around us. But as it radiates out, it usually glues itself to something or somebody—like a suction cup affixing itself to an object. This attachment of our life force onto an external object is what makes desire feverish and excruciating.

After all, we never really have that much control over any of the most important things in life—least of all other people.

We simply cannot control how they respond to us or how much they will desire us in return. So when our wanting attaches itself to other people and what they do, this puts us at their mercy: Our emotional state becomes subject to their whims. We feel helpless, and the mind spins feverishly, trying to figure out how to get them to give us what we need.

At the same time, fixating on another person pulls us out of ourselves, disrupting our connection with our own ground and vital center. Since this creates intense feelings of helplessness and disempowerment, it's not surprising that many people wind up shutting down their desire and need altogether.

It is this addictive quality of desire—where the life force becomes locked onto an external object—that many religious teachings warn against. This unbearable tension is what the Buddha was referring to when he said, "The cause of suffering is desire."

For many years I had trouble with this statement of the Buddha's. I could certainly see that clinging to objects of attachment caused painful states of obsession and addiction. But I found something missing in this formulation because it was clear to me that desire also contains real power and intelligence, that it can move mountains and is, finally, the energy that propels us to make intimate contact with life and move in the direction we are meant to go. I also did not want to forego letting myself fall passionately in love or feeling deep bonding with loved ones. I had found that the pure energy of desire, if experienced directly, without straining for fulfillment, had a luminous radiance and beauty of its own. It was the juice of life itself.

It took me years to sort out this seeming contradiction and to understand how desire could be the source of both endless suffering and great bliss. The key was in recognizing that desire can come in a whole spectrum of different forms—from crude to subtle, from feverish to sublime—depending on how tightly it is attached to an external object or fixed outcome.

At one end of the spectrum is desire at its most crude—what the Buddha called *craving*. This becomes especially destructive when it takes the form of a coercive demand or ultimatum: "Do what I want, or else . . . I'll leave you . . . I'll punish you . . . we'll bomb you back to the Stone Age." A more polite form of craving is the pressure-filled plea: "Please give me this, please, please, please."

Less extreme is ordinary, conventional desire—plainly wanting or needing something. Though less coercive than ultimatums, demands, and pleas, ordinary desire also creates stress and tension when it expects or requires a set, preconceived form of fulfillment, which is in fact beyond our control.

At the subtler end of the spectrum, when desire is no longer a suction cup grasping onto a fixed outcome, it can be experienced as passionate aliveness or even pure bliss. This is one of the profound secrets that comes from the Tantric traditions of the East. The key to making friends with your wanting is to center your attention within the energy of the desire itself, rather than on trying to control the object of desire or extract fulfillment from it.

When you find yourself in the grip of raw need, lust, craving, or obsession, you can learn to turn your attention away from the object of desire and toward the desire itself, as a feeling in your body. Then you can try to meet it with unconditional presence, as described in the previous two chapters. Notice how the intense energy of hunger or passion moves in your body, open yourself to that movement, and ride this energy by centering your awareness within it. Riding this energy is like a surfer learning to stand up on a roaring wave. You are at one with the power of the wave, and this feels blissful.

If riding desire is like surfing a wave, being carried away by desire is like being tossed around by the currents. This is a subtle but crucial difference, similar to the distinction between conscious and unconscious suffering. You're dealing with the same energy whether you relate to it consciously or not. But in conscious desire or conscious suffering, you enter into the experience with awareness, so that it doesn't overwhelm you, knocking the ground out from under you and sweeping you away. You have a conscious, deliberate experience of the desire and how it moves through you.

Through experiencing the pure energy of desire, you may then discover its subtler nature as radiant aliveness, which might feel passionate, powerful, and electric, or tender, delicate, and sweet. While desire fixated outwardly generates grasping and tension, desire inwardly felt attunes you to the pulsing power of the body's vital center.

Once you can ride the wave of desire, it runs its course and subsides. Then you may discover what is deeper than this pulsing energy. Just as the clear, calm depths of the ocean lie still below the thrashing waves, so the heart's pure longing to connect is what underlies our passion. This longing has its own intelligence, for it is a direct knowing that you grow and prosper only through being deeply in touch—with yourself, with others, and with life itself.

Even the Buddha, in an advanced teaching, had to acknowledge that "desire is perfectly pure." Desire is perfectly pure in the way that fire is: It is simply blazing energy, not something intrinsically harmful. It takes a destructive form only when we handle it wrongly. If we can uncover the deeper longing contained in this radiant heat, it can bring about an inner melting that opens up our capacity to let love enter fully into us.

The Good Other and the Sacred Thou

When craving carries us away and we imagine that another person is *the one* who can bring total fulfillment at last, we are projecting onto that person the image of the "good other." If the bad other is the one we resent for not giving us what we need, the good other is the one we imagine will make everything okay by loving us in just the right way. While the bad-other image is colored by fear, fashioned out of past hurt and disappointment, the good-other image is colored by hope, fashioned out of the longing for perfect love. So when other people feel us projecting this inflated image onto them, they usually recoil, knowing they cannot possibly meet our need.

Popular love songs are full of these godlike projections: "You are everything and everything is you." "I can't live if living is without you." "You are my sunshine, my only sunshine."

But think about it for a moment. What would it really be like to live with someone who is everything, your only source of sunshine, the whole foundation of your existence? You would find yourself in the position of Majnun, the lover in a famous Sufi tale who literally goes mad for his beloved Layla, crying out, "I follow obediently my beloved, who owns my soul." In modern terms, that would be a sign of disempowerment, codependence, emotional fusion, and addiction. In giving Layla his soul, Majnun has lost connection with his own vital center.

Yet I must admit that even though I understand this rationally, there is also a place in me that resonates with and responds powerfully to the grand sentiments in these love songs. And I've always loved the tale of Layla and Majnun and others like it. Does this mean I'm just a hopeless romantic, addicted to the dream of the ideal lover who will bring perfect fulfillment and soothe all my cares away? Or is there some deeper, underlying truth contained in sentiments like "you are everything and everything is you"?

Recently I looked over all the love poems I'd written to different women in my life, collected over the course of thirty-five years. Even though these women are all quite distinct in my mind, each possessing her own particular beauty and woundedness, I noticed that the passion and longing in each of these poems seemed to be addressed to one and the same special *you*.

One poem, using the metaphor of a dry landscape whose creek beds swell with the first rains of the season, ends with the line, "All my streams run to you." Even now it's not hard for me to resonate with the feeling in that line, that sweet surrender of the gravitational pull that *you*—the special *you,* whose luminous presence inspires awe and wonder—exert on me.

Yet what exactly is this magnetic pull? If I imagine that the other person possesses some special power or magic that I am missing and *must have* at any cost, then addiction takes over, as I obsess over what this "good other" can bestow on me. But if instead I look at what is happening inside me, I recognize the influence of the beloved as something like that of an exquisite passage of music, as it draws me into a fresh, unknown space where I taste a certain depth of soul. On being moved by a sublime passage from Beethoven, I might conclude that I should listen to Beethoven every day. But it's not really about Beethoven. Yes, Beethoven is magnificent, as is the one I love, but the real power and magic lie in what is stirred within me.

Passion and longing, then, are my responses to the sacred *you*—which could take the form of a lover, a mountain at dusk, or the *Moonlight Sonata*—you who allow me to enter into the mystery of my own being. As expressed in a poem I once wrote after a painful heartbreak:

> Who is this *you* I want?
> *You* is just a name tag—
> For greater being which is all around,
> And inside too.

This is what Rumi means when he declares, "The one I love is everywhere." *The you I love is everywhere*: in the snowflakes falling, in the eyes that reveal my beloved's inner light, or in the lovely wave of passion welling up from within the vital center.

Thus the sentiment in romantic pop songs grows from the same root as that of the great devotional poetry in the spiritual traditions. In traditional religious terms, it is the soul's longing for God. After all, it is only to God, or the mysterious source of all, that we can truly sing, "you are everything and everything is you." It is only to absolute love that we can rightfully declare, "you are my sunshine, my only sunshine," and "I can't live if living is without you." Our longing for the source of love is as natural as a deer's thirst for water. Or in the lovely phrasing of the Psalmbook: "Like as the hart desireth the waterbrooks, so longeth my soul after Thee, O Lord."

Many great mystics and sages have found that the thirst for God is most fully satisfied through drinking from the wellspring of spirit that flows within our very core. Some spiritual traditions, such as Sufism, see longing as a direct tap-line into absolute love because it provides that inner moistening. When the great Sufi mystic Ibn al-'Arabī exclaims, "O Lord, nourish me not with love, but with the longing for love," he is recognizing that longing deeply felt is nourishing in itself. For it rouses the heart, directly awakening us to what is most alive within us.

In this same vein Rumi sings:

Hear the dog as it cries for its master:
That crying *is* the connection.

Rumi is telling us that the longing that wells up from deep within is not just a need for external gratification, but a direct link to our "master"—the great richness hidden within us, which the Tibetans call the wish-fulfilling gem. In the words of the Indian teacher Nisargadatta, "Desire is devotion . . . to the real, to the infinite, the eternal heart of being." And therefore, "it is not desire that is wrong, but [only] its narrowness and smallness." Interestingly, the Tibetan term for devotion is composed of two words combined: longing and humbleness. Longing is like the arrow of a compass magnetically directing us to the source of love, while humbleness is the openness that invites love to come streaming in.

Infinite Passion

One of the most frustrating things about relationships is that we always seem to want more from them than they offer. Even if you do manage to win the object of your desire, you are never entirely satisfied with him or her, isn't this so? You would like your beloved to be more beautiful, more sexy, more attuned, more attentive, more responsive, more . . . "Well, maybe this isn't the right person after all," you may eventually conclude. Yet even when we finally decide that someone is the right person, he or she still never seems totally right in every way.

It's curious and amusing, isn't it? You feel attracted to someone, you woo and pursue, you win this person over, you make love, and maybe you finally marry. But somehow none of that puts an end to your longing. Your passion still wants something more. So then you may try having kids— maybe that's the fulfillment that will satisfy your yearning. Or you try to perform a makeover on your partner, so that he or she will finally do it for you. But that creates more problems, so then you might try couples therapy or take up workshops on Tantric sex. Yet no matter how much things may improve, your longing for something more never entirely disappears.

But this is not a problem! It's not a sign that something is wrong with you for wanting more or with your beloved for failing to satisfy all your desires. We can only make peace with the endlessness of our passion through recognizing the true object of our desire.

Desire focused on a person can never be totally satisfied. That's because the one we love stirs our passion for something that lies beyond this finite person. Kierkegaard called this "infinite passion," or "passion for the infinite."

Other animals, being totally rooted in the finite, are satisfied with immediate gratification of basic needs. But since human consciousness has roots in the infinite, we can discover in the beauty of finite things a much larger beauty shining through them. Our longing for more arises from what is infinite within us, and it aims for the infinite—boundless openness and love. It's never just this woman that I love. It's also the way she suggests and reveals a larger beauty beyond herself, sparking an expansive opening in me that lets me touch the beauty right here within myself. No theory of human love can ever be complete without this understanding.

Your longing is holy because it wants to link you up with the infinite source of all, as it lives within you. That is why, if you can open yourself to the energy of longing itself, it will take you beyond gross craving and attachment. Through your longing—the feeling that you cannot live if living is without true love—you turn toward love at its living source.

At bottom, you want yourself. Not a shrunken, superficial version of yourself but what is most real and alive in you. You want to feel your own juice, the elixir of great love flowing in your veins.

Of course, we often imagine that a new and more beautiful lover is what will give us this juice. That's understandable, especially if we feel turned on and juicy in someone's presence, or even just thinking about him or her. That's fine. There's no problem with the poetry of "you are my sunshine." It's delightful to write passionate poems to one's beloved, the sacred Thou, and to feel turned on by the play of sensuality.

But if we don't want to become enslaved, burned out, let down, or disenchanted, we must not become too serious about all of this. We need to bring greater awareness to our passion. This means realizing that the perfect lover of our dreams—the one who could lead us into a space of endless beauty and delight—can only be found, in truth, when we surrender to the very heart of life, the open expanse of being, hidden within this and every moment. Recognizing this will help free us from addiction to any person or relationship. Conscious passion means owning our desire-energy as our own living juice, and learning to ride on this wave of radiant aliveness.

The Indian teacher Sri Poonja once said wisely, "The desire

for freedom arises from freedom itself." The desire he is speaking of here is holy longing—the deep wish to connect with the essence of what you are. Indeed, you can want only what you've already had some taste of. You can't want an orange unless you know what an orange tastes like. And you can only yearn for freedom when you know what freedom feels like.

In the same way, we long for perfect love only because we've already had a taste of it. And since we haven't located it in the external world, our knowledge of perfect love can only have come from deep within ourselves. The longing for perfect love arises from perfect love itself, which dwells within the human heart.

It's as though we have a whole pantheon of gods and goddesses locked up inside us, hidden away in the depths of our being. There is the god of love, the goddess of beauty, the god of truth, the goddess of wisdom. If we listen intently, we can just barely hear them calling to us. They want to join with us and offer us everything, but we have been facing away from them for so long that it is hard to hear or recognize their faint cries. Yet their call can still be heard in the voice of our longing.

Seeking perfect love from imperfect relationships leaves us frustrated because it leads in the wrong direction. Since the desire for perfect love comes from perfect love itself, we need only follow the golden thread of our longing back to its source. In opening to the energy of passion and longing, we make ourselves receptive to a visit from the gods.

Opening to Receive

To sum this up in practical terms: Start simply, right from your longing to feel loved or your desire for something more from some relationship in your life. Maybe you want your partner to really understand you. Maybe you want to have someone come along and notice your beauty or see who you are. Maybe you want to feel more connected with someone. Maybe you long for happiness, ease, and well-being. Maybe you want better sex. Start from there.

Then gradually turn your attention from *what* you want toward the desire or need itself. What does your desire actually feel like as a living experience in your body? At first it may take a little effort and intention to turn your focus around like this. The key point is to *feel the desire or longing itself,* as it vibrates in your body. Maybe you have never paid much attention to this before. Pay particular attention to the vital center, in your belly, just below the navel. Take time to feel into it.

As you feel into your longing for love and connection, notice what it puts you in touch with. Don't think about this with your mind, but simply look at and feel what is there. You might feel some warmth or softening, some expansiveness or fullness, or a tingling sense of the body coming alive. One person in one of my workshops described it as "my heart bursting open more and more."

Sometimes there is a sweet sadness that comes with the longing as well. This is a soul sadness that grows out of recognizing how long we have felt separate and disconnected. It is a moisturizing sadness that softens the defensive shell around the heart, a purifying sadness that clears the ground for new life to spring up. It is an experience of grievance melting down into grief. Rumi calls this the "secret cup" because it makes us a vessel that is open to receiving:

The grief you cry out from
Draws you to union.

Your pure sadness
That wants help
Is the secret cup.

Whether or not it is accompanied by this soul sadness, opening directly to your longing makes you more pliable and receptive. As it brings you into your body, your vital center, and your heart, you may find that love is not all that far away. Perhaps it has already secretly entered the room.

Love Wants You

Opening to our longing unveils the subtlest of all forms of desire: prayer. Just as longing is a subtler form of desire than craving, so prayer is subtler still. It is a pure connecting with what is most real—the openness and warmth from which all blessings flow.

The pure wish to be one with love is the eternal prayer that lives within the heart. This prayer also lies hidden within our desire for another person's love. In wanting to be loved, we want the experience of *love coming toward us*. The truth is, the benevolence in this universe is always coming toward us and shining upon us, like the light of the sun. Countless people have discovered this through finding grace and blessings in the most difficult, even the most horrific circumstances. The key lies in *letting* love come toward us. This is what Rumi means when he says, "To find the beloved, you must become the beloved." We become the beloved by opening up to let love in.

In a small way, this is what happened to Julie when she let Rick see how much she wanted him. The grief she cried out from drew her to union. Without even knowing what she was doing, she let her longing come forward and be seen, and this invited love into the room. At that point neither Julie nor Rick had all that much choice in the matter.

Julie did not decide to reveal herself. Instead, her usual defenses fell away, like a cloak sliding off her shoulders, allowing Rick to see her standing naked before him. Nor did Rick decide to respond as he did. He couldn't help it. His heart was simply responding to the one he loved when she no longer turned her face away from him. The clouds parted and a ray of pure love shone through him choicelessly, at least for that moment.

Holy longing is the secret cup that invites love to enter into us. In this sense, we could say that genuine receiving can be an even more sacred act than giving—because it requires humbling ourselves and melting open, giving up control, and making ourselves fully available to love as the great power that infuses us with life.

When you become the secret cup, it's not just you wanting love anymore. Instead, you find that *love wants you*. It has only been waiting for you to let it in. When you lay bare your holy longing, then, as Rumi counsels, "miraculous beings come running to help."

CHAPTER SIX

The Love That Sets You Free

Love is always loving you.

—H. W. L. POONJA

OUR BIRTHRIGHT as human beings is to have direct access to perfect love, and our privilege is to serve as a channel through which it flows. Realizing this, we can see the folly of trying to earn love through efforts, looks, or achievements. We might be able to win approval, praise, or rewards by these means, but not the love that embraces us as we are, the love that sets us free, the love that lights up this world. Rather than trying to win love, we need to let it fully enter into us.

How can we let this happen, so that we can know we are loved absolutely, and know this with certainty, in our flesh and bones?

Absolute Love, Here and Now

I would like to present a simple yet powerful way to connect directly with the living presence of absolute love that is always available. I am not sure whether to call this a practice, an invocation, or a prayer. However you like to think of it, the essence of it is to tune in experientially to the immediate presence of love, through activating the longing that already exists within your heart, as discussed in the previous chapter. Please do not try to direct this process with your mind or concentrate too narrowly on the words that follow. It is best to do this at a time when you can settle down and let your mind relax.

This practice will help you open up the receiving channels in your body and start to experience the absolute love that is ever present. The suggestions that follow are simply guidelines that I have found helpful, both for myself and in working with others. You might try following them closely at first and then eventually adapt them in your own way.

1. Settle into your body.

Take a few moments to sit quietly and settle down. You may prefer to lie down. Start by coming down out of your mind and inhabiting your body. You might take a few deep breaths and feel the sensations of aliveness in different parts of your body. Sense your vital center in the belly, three finger-widths below your navel. This is where you can feel your connection with the earth most fully. Breathe into the belly and ground yourself there. Feel your heart center, in the middle of your chest. This is where you can feel your connection with your humanness most fully, with its tenderness, warmth, and compassion. Then sense the crown center, at the top and rear of your head. This is the heaven center, where you are oriented toward the infinite. Sense how these three centers line up in a vertical column of bodily presence.

2. ACKNOWLEDGE YOUR SEPARATION FROM LOVE.

Then turn your attention toward some way in which you feel cut off or separate from love in your life right now, and let yourself acknowledge that. You might think of a specific person who doesn't love you as much as you'd like, or a more general way in which you feel love missing. Then take a moment to see how the lack of love feels in your body. Perhaps it appears as an emptiness, a hole, a deadness, a loneliness, or a fear. Let yourself feel that directly. This is important because feeling the absence of love helps activate your longing for it. Stay close to the bodily felt experience as much as possible, without letting your mind manufacture a whole story about it.

3. FEEL THE ENERGY OF YOUR LONGING.

Once you sense your separation from love, an impulse to do something to fix it may arise. After all, we have all developed strategies for winning love, admiration, or approval to ease this feeling of separation. We may try to prove ourselves, or to please, charm, or impress others. We might complain, demand, or even sulk, hoping that others will come after us. If any of these impulses arises right now, just notice it and come back to simply feeling the separation from love, without trying to do anything about it.

While paying attention to the sense of separation, see if you can notice any longing to feel more connected with love. Let yourself acknowledge how much you want to experience pure love, how much you want to be seen, understood, appreciated, and accepted—in short, to be held in love, to be loved as you are.

Now let yourself open to the pure energy of this wish or longing, without focusing on trying to get anything from anybody in particular. Feel the energy contained in the longing, and let your attention rest in this bodily feeling. Sense the natural desire of the heart to abide in great love. This longing is sacred because it is an entry into truth, the truth of your heart as an open channel through which love naturally wants to flow.

4. OPEN THE HEART AND CROWN CENTERS.

See if you can feel the longing in your heart center, in the middle of your chest. Let that whole area be filled with the energy of your longing. Let yourself enter deeper and deeper into that feeling. As the energy of the longing stirs, notice any way your heart seems to open or come alive. Also let your crown center, at the top and back of your head, become soft and receptive. Feel this receptive openness in both the heart and the crown centers.

(If you have trouble feeling your heart center, breathe gently into it. As you breathe or tune in to the heart, you may begin to sense it as an open, energized space. If you need further help feeling your heart center, you can put your hands over the center of your chest while thinking of something or someone you deeply appreciate. If you have trouble feeling the crown center, sense the space directly above it and the connection between that space and the top of the head.)

5. LET YOURSELF RECEIVE.

Notice how there is, contained in your longing, a desire to receive love. Feel and acknowledge that yes to receiving. What that yes is essentially saying is, "I want to let you enter me."

As you experience that openness to receiving, then look and see: Is there any presence of love at hand right now? Don't think about it or look too hard. Rather, sense this very softly, very subtly: Is the presence of love available right now, is it anywhere at hand? Don't imagine or fabricate anything with your mind. Don't make it up. Simply experience what's there.

If there is some sense of warmth or love at hand, let it enter you. Don't try to make anything happen. Let your body be totally receptive; let your pores drink in the warmth that's there. Feel the cells of your body bathing in the presence of love.

Notice how the presence of love is not something located in only one spot. It is more like a gentle breeze softly holding, surrounding, or permeating you. Let yourself be held in the space of great love and see what that feels like. To whatever extent any sense of openness, warmth, or tenderness is there, see how it feels to let it move through or fill your body.

(If you don't feel any presence of love, then most likely you didn't feel your separation from it or your longing for it strongly enough. In that case, you could try saying one or more phrases gently to yourself while experiencing how they're true for you, such as: "I want to feel loved," "I want to feel held in love," "I want to know that I am loved," or "I want to let love in." Don't say these words as a form of autosuggestion or affirmation, but as a way to make your deep wish and prayer more consciously felt. See how it affects you to state your wish in words while *feeling* its truth.)

Give yourself plenty of time to be with whatever you're experiencing. The presence of absolute love can be very subtle; it usually doesn't announce itself in dramatic ways. It might feel like being infused with warmth, or surrounded by a soft plasma, or held in a gentle embrace. It might feel like floating in a pool of warm water or simply like total relaxation and stillness.

You may find that your mind resists, or you become distracted by thoughts, or you may not trust what is happening. You may think that you are making the whole thing up. Just notice these mental games without struggling with them. Remember that the ego has made a habit of resisting love because it is afraid of melting. It doesn't trust that if it lets down its defenses, love could just be there in a reliable way. So if you encounter any resistance in this process, hold it in a kind and gentle way.

6. LET YOURSELF MELT AND LET LOVE HOLD YOU.

Feeling the presence of love, let yourself relax and melt into it. Instead of having to hold yourself up, let yourself be held by love instead. Soften the boundaries of the body, and feel what it is like to melt into this warmth. Notice the effect this has on your body, and stay present with that subtle feeling.

Can you feel love as a gentle presence that holds and enfolds you, allowing you to relax and let go? You don't have to hold yourself up. Let love be your ground.

I would suggest trying this practice regularly at first, perhaps while lying in bed first thing in the morning or last thing at night. After you have found your way with it, then you can also do the practice very briefly, in a minute or two, and find nourishment and renewal in that.

When I first discovered this practice, through my own personal need for it, I was surprised by how concretely I could feel the presence of love entering and infusing my body. This experience was fairly subtle, rather than anything dramatic. Above all, it required an ability to open and let in the nourishment that is right here in this very moment. This nourishing presence was not something I could hold on to; I could only stay open and let it enter me.

As I continued working with this practice, I felt profound changes happening. I experienced a new kind of trust and relaxation in knowing that I could have my own direct access to perfect love whenever I needed it. My investment in grievance diminished, along with tendencies to expect others to provide ideal love.

Yet though at first it seemed I would never go back to needing love from people in the same way again, I did eventually find myself slipping back into old relational expectations. Nonetheless, the absolute-love practice left me with a new, concrete knowledge that something else was possible, and this served as a polestar in guiding me toward seeing what I still needed to work on to free myself further.

I say this so that you will not become discouraged if you find yourself slipping back after having some new realizations with this practice. Since most growth happens in the form of "two steps forward, one step back," slipping back doesn't mean your experience of absolute love was just an illusion.

Living in Love

Through opening to absolute love in this way, many people in my workshops have also discovered that the love they most long for is directly available. As a man in one of my groups described this, "I am amazed to discover that if I feel my longing for love deeply enough, that is the same as feeling the love itself. As soon as I feel the longing, the love is right there at the same time. I feel a sense of warmth and flow, filling up and overflowing." His finding accords with the words from the Bible:

"Ask and it shall be given, seek and ye shall find, knock and it shall be opened unto you." Asking in this case means consciously experiencing the heart's true longing, which opens up a clear channel that invites absolute love to enter.

People experience the presence of absolute love in different ways. One woman felt it as "a spaciousness, not necessarily warm, just spacious." She is feeling the open dimension of absolute love, which doesn't necessarily have the warm and fuzzy quality of human contact. Another woman experienced it as "a beautiful sweetness drizzling down on me." Another woman felt "a lot of intense light and warmth and bliss." Another spoke of looking at first for some kind of ecstasy, but finding instead that love's presence was "very simple. There wasn't a lot of emotion; it was more clear and neutral. And there was a sense of equilibrium, like being held up by water."

One man said: "The love that is there when I open in this way is not coming from somewhere or going somewhere. It's nondirectional—just a simple, open presence." Another man spoke of "a fullness that made me feel more alive." Another described it as "a powerful experience of being known, which feels like the resolution of my grievance about not feeling seen." Here are other words that people have used to portray the influx of love: "soft," "still," "radiating," "inclusive," "energizing," "animating," "grounding," "restful."

One woman spoke of the humor in her discovery: "What a joke: the love I've been hungering for was right here all the time. I can't believe how much pain I have put myself through imagining that love is missing and that I have to extract it from someone! But now I see that all I have to do is to tune my receiver and there it is. It seems as though love is always ready to respond: 'I have only been waiting all this time for you to turn your face toward me and let me hear your call.'"

Just as fish do not see the water around them, so we mostly fail to recognize the ocean of love that surrounds and holds us up. Though love is inside and all around, it is so fine and transparent that, like water, it often seems invisible. So all our lives we have been trying to win love, not realizing that great love is right here, freely available. We have been trying to hold ourselves up, not realizing that love is the ever-present ground supporting our whole existence. We have been trying to prove we are worthy of love, while failing to realize that our very nature is already lovely and lovable.

As long as you still hold onto the childhood fixation on not being loved, then no matter how much others love you, it will never be enough. The wound will operate like a hole in you: No matter how much love someone pours in, it will always leak out the bottom. And you will continue focusing on the love that's not there rather than the love that is. That is why the practice of tuning in to absolute love is so important. It is a way out of the endless, fruitless attempt to plug the hole of love from outside.

As soon as you fully acknowledge your thirst, the waters of love find an opening and start flowing toward you. At first it seems as though love is coming to you from somewhere outside. But as you let love's subtle presence enter you, you can no longer say that I am here and love is there, two separate things. There is no separation.

To know that you are loved, then, is to know that you *are* love. When you let down your defenses and allow love to pour into you, you become one with love, like a sheet of ice melting into the river from which it came. Just as the ice was never separate from the river, so the freezing of the heart has only created a temporary separation from your nature as love.

Melting into love is what the soul has always wanted. The

relief it brings goes much deeper than just outgrowing childhood pain. It heals the universal spiritual wound of separation from love.

This is what we usually seek, whether we know it or not, in our fantasy of the perfect partner—someone in whose arms we could completely let go and relax. What is orgasm, after all, but this? We simply cannot help seeking perfect love, for it is what will help us melt into the warm expanse of openness that is our very nature. "To find the beloved, you must become the beloved" means becoming one with the love that is always loving us.

The theistic traditions describe this as becoming "the beloved of God" or "a child of God." In the words of an English hymn:

> Come down, O love divine,
> Seek thou this soul of mine.

Nontheistic traditions like Buddhism state it differently: "Your mind is one with the compassion and wisdom of all the buddhas." Yet whatever the language or belief, the great saints and sages of all times always exude great love and compassion, for their heart is one with the absolute love in which they swim. In becoming the beloved, who they are is no longer separate from love.

The defensive ego is like floorboards we put under our feet to hold us up when we do not trust that love is holding us. Yet though this self-constructed flooring can provide a sense of security, it also separates us from the larger open ground of our being. To let love in, we need to start opening up spaces between the floorboards so that love's warmth can rise up and envelop us.

The Work and Play of Relationship

If you received a phone call telling you that you'd just won a million dollars in a lottery, and then you walked outside and discovered that someone had just stolen your car, it probably wouldn't bother you too much. Similarly, discovering that you have direct access to great love starts to put the frustrations and disappointments of human love into perspective. You become less dependent on family, friends, or lovers for approval, which is, after all, but a poor substitute for the real thing. Then you can begin to stand on your own and dare to be yourself in a relationship. And since you are less tempted to sell yourself out to win love, there is less resentment.

After discovering their own access to the source of love, participants in my groups sometimes ask: "If you can open to absolute love directly, it seems like you wouldn't need people as much anymore. Couldn't this lead to devaluing or turning away from intimate relationship altogether?" This is not an idle question, as many people today have made the choice as they grow older to live alone. And others have decided that relationships and their difficulties are a distraction from the spiritual path or an impediment to their spiritual well-being.

This whole question of needing other people is a confusing and tricky one. Although having access to the source of love can reduce emotional neediness, it is not exactly a substitute for human warmth and connectedness. While this book has focused on how to heal ourselves—by bringing ourselves back to life in the places we're wounded and shut down—healthy relationships can also play an important part in this healing. A helping relationship like psychotherapy, a devotional bond with a spiritual master, or a deep soul connection with a friend or lover can provide an important corrective experience that opens our capacity to let love move through us.

Yet even when a relationship functions in this positive way, it's important to remember that true nourishment, growth, and expansion come about only through what happens within us, in how we learn to soften and open our guarded heart. Looking to someone else to fill our holes or always satisfy our passion only cuts us off from the wellspring of beauty and power within.

The point of accessing absolute love directly is not to disengage from relationships. Instead, it allows us to inhabit them more fully, with greater presence and potency. The less I depend on the one I love to fill my holes, the more freely I can see her as she is, show myself as I am, and brave the risks of real intimacy. When my partner and I lay down the frustrating burden of trying to extract perfect love and acceptance from each other, we can see our relationship in a new light: as a field of work and play that provides an opportunity to grow and transform through each other's influence.

THE WORK OF RELATIONSHIP

As we have seen throughout this book, just because we are fashioned out of absolute love, this does not mean that we can embody it very fully in our relationships. Nothing stretches our capacity to embody great love like learning to accept others in all of their differences and limitations, especially when these trigger our emotional hot spots. There is nothing like a relationship to show us where we are frozen and shut down, where we have trouble making contact, where we are most afraid, and where we refuse to accept what is. Nothing else so quickly brings our core wound to the surface, exposing all the ways we still feel unloved or unlovable. Human relationships provide the ultimate litmus test of how healed, or whole, or spiritually mature we really are.

Usually when we shut down in relationships, it is because the other person's emotional wounds have activated wounds of our own that we cannot tolerate. My partner's anger, for instance, may trigger my deep fear of rejection. If I can't handle that fear, then I close down when she is angry. So to stay open and present with the one I love in difficult moments, I must be able to hold my own emotional trigger-points in awareness and kind understanding. If I can handle my fear, then I can handle her anger.

Healing the love-wound doesn't mean it has been banished forever; instead, it means gaining some freedom from its influence over us. We develop this freedom through a process of understanding and unfolding like the one described in this book—which allows us to pause and consider what is happening when our wound is triggered, instead of just discharging some automatic emotional reaction. Every time I shut down to someone, this is an opportunity to face my woundedness and see where I am shut down in myself as well. This willingness to face my own shutdown is the key that allows me to stay open, both to myself and to the one who is triggering my pain. Through learning to accept what is hardest to accept in myself, I gain the fortitude to face what seems most impossible in my partner and to offer her genuine kindness and caring when she most needs it.

If my partner and I can learn to speak together about the wounded places that give rise to our emotional reactions, this will also help us remain more awake when the wounds are triggered. Until recently, couples never had access to language or psychological understandings that would allow them to talk about the complex feelings they stirred in each other. And this limited how much they could share of themselves, one with the other. Awareness of each other's woundedness around loving and being loved helps a relationship deepen and become more resilient and intimate.

Through making peace with the wound my partner triggers in me, as well as with her wound, which I trigger in turn, I become much more accepting of myself and her. This is why consciously working with the wound of the heart is not a narcissistic self-indulgence. Coming to terms with our woundedness helps us navigate the complex emotional dynamics of human relationship and gradually bring a more all-embracing love into this world.

With this kind of perspective we can begin to see and appreciate the hidden perfection or sacred meaning contained within all the imperfection and turmoil of human relationship. Learning to ride the turbulent ups and downs of relative love makes us more tolerant, more understanding, more humble, more wise. Thus all the storms and trials of relationship serve a useful function, bending and shaping us so that we become a clearer, more open channel through which unconditional love can flow.

Authentic loving presence—the meeting of I and Thou—requires me to be able to honor all of my own experience and all of yours at the same time: not denying any of my experience or yours, not denying the differences between the two, and respecting these differences while feeling the rawness of never being able to fully overcome my aloneness and share my world with you. Yet still letting the longing for human contact forever arise anew, again and again, and ripple through me—the longing to reach out, to let in, to touch, and to taste the joy of letting myself feel drawn toward you, the sacred other, the luminous unknown.

The Play of Relationship

Wonderful as it is to receive love directly from the absolute source, this in no way diminishes the special delight and significance of sharing its human expression as it sparkles through a smile, a look, or the energetic contact of hearts, minds, and hands. Indeed, intimate, personal love is not just a pale reflection of absolute love, but a further expression of it. After all, the absolute source does not have expressive eyes we can gaze into, filling us with warmth and tenderness. And only two human bodies can share all the nuances of naked touch and feel. Only in sexual play do the two poles of existence—spirit and body, masculine and feminine, heaven and earth, beauty and beast—join in full-bodied union. Only two persons can speak the sacred words "I see your beauty" or "I love you for who you are." Soulful, personal love—the capacity to cherish and respond to the unique beauty of another, who in turn responds to our unique beauty—is a joy few worldly pleasures can match.

Many spiritual teachers, such as Krishnamurti, are willing to give the name *love* only to pure, selfless love, as though relative love, with all its fluctuating passions, were unworthy of the name. Selfless, unconditional openness is certainly love's essence and highest possibility. As the most refined, subtle frequency of love, the pure expression of spirit, it is like the ultraviolet end of the light spectrum—pure white light.

Yet love is also a wide-spectrum light with many shades and hues, ranging from ultraviolet—the openness of pure spirit—to infrared—the warmth of bodily and emotional contact. Since human beings are not pure spirit alone, the infrared heat of personal and sexual intimacy can help tune and enliven body and soul as instruments of deeper resonance. Through embodied human love the divine takes up residence on this earth.

Caring for Others

Having explored intimate relationship as a transformative journey in my books *Journey of the Heart* and *Love and Awakening*, I wanted in this book to focus instead on our inmost connection to love itself and the disconnection from it that has left our world so broken and torn apart. This focus has led me to emphasize the central importance of being able to receive love in healing the wound of the heart.

Yet in truth, receiving and giving are both equally essential, for they are the inhalation and exhalation of the breath of love. Knowing that we are *loved,* as we have seen, can help us discover that we *are* love. And this sets us free—*to* love, to care for others as *they* are, apart from our designs on them. The more we "become the beloved"—through letting the sun of absolute love shine upon us—the more this ripens our capacity to embody unconditional love in the world around us.

This whole cycle—accessing pure, absolute love and giving forth human caring and kindness—corresponds to two great commandments upon which Christ said "the whole Law and the Prophets depend." The first is to love God with all one's heart, soul, mind, and strength. As a child, I had a hard time understanding what this meant when I first heard about it in Sunday school. How was I—this small, impoverished creature who barely recognized the presence of love within me—supposed to send love to God, the almighty Father, who didn't even need my love anyway because He already is and has everything? Although I was told that I *should* do this, I had no idea what it meant or how to go about it. Certainly no one at Sunday school ever suggested that you might have a hard time with the first commandment if you did not know that you were truly loved yourself.

Through the practice of opening to absolute love, I came to understand Christ's first commandment in a more concrete, immediate way. If the presence of absolute love is "nondirectional," as one of my students described it, this means it is not something that a self over here gives to God over there, or that God out there gives to a self over here. To love God with all one's heart must mean immersing oneself in the all-pervasive stream of absolute love that *is* God. When immersed in this stream of blessing, I can see that love is not something I give or am given. It is the essential substance of what I am, my whole heart, mind, and strength. Loving God with all my heart and mind must mean loving my very nature as love itself, opening into pure openness, like water poured into water.

Christ's further commandment, to "love thy neighbor as thyself," arises directly out of discovering this love that lives within you. When you know yourself *as* openness and warmth, this sensitizes you to the pain of others who feel shut down and cut off from these qualities. You can see, behind their fear and defenses, that they too are desperate to know and connect with something beautiful and real within themselves. And then loving your neighbor—through sharing the wealth, this gift of warmth and openness—becomes more possible.

The Buddha understood the relation between absolute love and human kindness in a similar way. The Buddhist term for perfect love is *awake heart*—the natural open presence of our true nature (absolute *bodhichitta* in Sanskrit). Residing in this open presence corresponds to loving God with all one's heart and mind in the Christian tradition. This connection with absolute love can have a "vertical" feeling to it, in that it almost seems to pour down from above as a stream of blessings—from God or the wisdom guru or the vast openness above the crown of the head. This inflow enters and energizes the heart center, which can then radiate "horizontally" as kindness and caring toward all sentient beings. This infrared radiation is relative awake heart (relative *bodhichitta*).

This vertical connection to skylike openness above straightens us up, metaphorically speaking, allowing for an upright, balanced posture in relating to others. As one of my students spoke of his realization after the absolute-love practice: "I felt myself straighten up. And I saw that trying to get love is like leaning over at an angle. When leaning like that, I lose the vertical connection to my own ground, and I become even more desperate to win love from out there." Straightening up like this allows us to practice genuine kindness, free of any ruse to make other people like us.

The Buddha knew that loving one's neighbor is often not so easy, even after opening to absolute love, for the habits of fear and grievance have etched well-worn grooves in our psyche that will continue to draw us into them unless we consciously practice relating to others in new ways. Thus the Buddhist tradition contains many practical methods for generating loving-kindness and compassion toward others.

One simple way to activate caring for others is to remember your own wish to know yourself as beautiful and lovable, and then to recognize that everyone without exception has this same wish, whether they know it or not. If you look deeply at your worst enemies and the desperadoes of the world like Stalin, Hitler, or bin Laden, you can recognize that behind their aggressive facades, they too have this wish—which they dare not reveal to anyone, least of all themselves. They judge themselves as weak for having this need and feel ashamed of it, hiding it behind a mask of pseudostrength. And so they come to deny and forget the deeper longing hidden beneath their drive for success, power, expertise, wealth, celebrity, or revenge.

When you see how ashamed your fellow humans are of their desire for love, regarding it as a weakness, something to hate themselves for, how does this affect you? How much we all hide the tenderness of our heart, so that no one can see it! As you contemplate this, a glimmer of compassion may arise for yourself and all beings who want to know happiness but continually keep it at bay.

Christ's two commandments are connected in another way as well: Boundless love cannot flow into us unless it also has an outlet that allows it to keep circulating. If opening to absolute love unclogs the in-channel, expressing tenderness and kindness unclogs the out-channel, clearing away old traces of grievance still blocking it. Even if we just start practicing kindness in little ways, such as letting someone go ahead of us in traffic or saying hello to strangers in a friendly voice, this exercises our heart, nourishing us in the process as well. For as the Indian teacher Sri Poonja points out, "When you love, you are loving your own heart."

Living for the Love of It

Knowing we are held in great love frees us from the status of beggars anxiously awaiting our next handout. This allows us to act more creatively and effectively in the world.

When we no longer secretly try to win love through our work, we become much better artists, businesspeople, politicians, parents, students, or teachers. We are freed to do what we do as a form of creative play rather than as a form of self-validation.

The same principle holds true in every sphere, from political leadership to spiritual practice. Given the great challenges facing our planet, there is a tremendous need for wise leaders who can, out of their love for humanity, put the long-term benefit of the planet above the short-term interest of their approval ratings.

In religious communities, one of the biggest obstacles to spiritual development is the secret agenda to win love through being a good parishioner, a serious meditator, or a hardworking disciple. Zealously trying to be nice, to meditate correctly, to pray sincerely, to devote themselves to their teacher or to service, people hope to win the recognition from God, the guru, or the community that they never received as a child. Yet all of this effort only leaves them with long, dour faces. Trying to win approval or acceptance is always a joyless task.

For many years I engaged in spiritual practice in the impoverished way I have just described. And for many of us it may be unavoidable to start that way. Although I found great benefit in meditation—greater awareness, greater understanding, greater compassion—it troubled me that I did not feel much delight in it. Though my life was good in most respects, I still lacked a deep sense of joy in my heart.

This lack of joy became my koan—a Zen-like riddle requiring an answer that could not come from my mind. For years I tried to find out what was missing, and I discovered many things about what was blocking my joy, important things I needed to look at. Yet none of this lifted the cloud from my heart.

It was not until I began to discover direct access to perfect love within myself that the sun finally began to come out from behind the clouds in a more consistent way. Joy arose from knowing that I was one with the presence of love and that I didn't have to prove or achieve anything to deserve that benevolence, because it was already built into the fabric of who I was.

From there I started to recognize the radiant energy of aliveness at the core of my being as intrinsically blissful or, in the words of the poet Blake, as "eternal delight." When love or passion flows unobstructedly, it is experienced as bliss. And when we awaken to the bliss in our veins, its natural outflow is radiant love.

Of course, in our creaturely vulnerability, there is no way to avoid loss and separation from what we love. We cannot avoid coming back again and again to the experience of being alone. No one can finally get inside our skin and share our experience—the nuances that we alone feel, the changes that we alone are going through, the death that we alone must die. Nonetheless, loss, separation, and this fundamental aloneness are important teachers, for they force us to take up residence in the only real home we have—the naked presence of the heart, which no external loss can destroy.

Standing in this, our own true ground, is the ultimate healing balm for the ache of separation and the wound of love. "You must fall in love with the one inside your heart," says the teacher Poonja. "Then you will see that it has always been there, but that you have wanted something else. To taste

bliss, forget all other tastes and taste the wine served within."
The warmth and openness at our core is the most intimate
beloved who is always present, and into whose arms we can
let go at last.

Epilogue
Who's Holding You?

Sarah was a highly intelligent and attractive woman I had worked with in therapy for several years. Having been through three marriages and many affairs, she desperately wanted to find a relationship she could finally settle into. Yet she had never been able to create one that worked for her.

Sarah's father had left the family when she was an infant, and her mother had married another man. Her mother never told her the truth, leading Sarah to believe that her mother's new husband was Sarah's real father. Throughout her childhood Sarah knew in her body that something was missing, but did not know what. In addition, her mother was not capable of taking care of Sarah's emotional needs, so Sarah wound up taking care of her mother instead. As a result, she came to believe that love was in short supply and that she had to earn every scrap that came her way.

Sarah continually enacted this belief in her relationships with men. She married men who were emotionally unavailable and had passionate affairs with men who had other commitments. Her tendency was to focus on what the man wanted while putting herself aside. As a result, though she was a beautiful soul, she had never found a man who saw or valued her enough to give her his all.

After much work on these issues, Sarah finally met someone who was crazy about her, and she about him. The only catch: Eric was still involved with another woman, whom he saw part-time and whose children he had helped raise. Although he deeply loved and wanted Sarah, his fear of the consequences of leaving the other woman prevented him from being able to commit to her 100 percent.

Sarah waited for Eric for several months, feeling excruciating torment whenever he was with the other woman. Finally she could not stand it any longer. She realized that she would have to stop seeing him if he could not break off with the other woman. While this was hard for her, she had gained enough self-respect through our work to know she had to do it. Yet no longer seeing Eric also brought up powerful waves of emotion, which allowed her to explore her core wounding more deeply than ever before.

Since this relationship was the closest Sarah had come to what she wanted with a man, Eric's inability to commit was totally devastating. She had tremendous anger about that, and I encouraged her to feel it fully. After working through the anger, she went into grief about having become involved, once again, in a relationship with someone who was not fully there for her.

As she opened to her grief, I asked her what was most painful for her, and she said, "Feeling so alone, and never being able to get my needs met." Then we explored what she was most needing, and she said, "I'm tired of trying so hard to get someone to love me. I want to know that someone can just be there for me, that I can relax and feel held for a change."

We were at a critical juncture. Sarah had never developed a nourishing relationship because she had never owned or fully allowed herself to feel her desire to be loved, with the vulnerability and endangerment that implied. It had always been much safer to focus on taking care of the man's needs instead, hoping he'd throw a few crumbs her way. This time was different. Sarah was finally acknowledging the depth of her longing to be held in love.

I encouraged Sarah to repeat the words "I want to feel held," and see how that affected her. As she did this, a warmth and softness began spreading throughout her body. The focus was no longer on Eric or her grief. Directly experiencing her deep longing to feel held allowed something in her to relax. And in relaxing she discovered a presence that actually seemed to be holding and supporting her. This had a profound effect on her. Her whole face softened into a smile and she was totally at peace.

After a while, I encouraged her to alter the words slightly—to see what it would be like to say, "I want to *let myself* feel held." While this phrasing was only slightly different, it put more emphasis on her willingness to open herself to that holding.

At first this was a bit too threatening for her. The change of phrase let her see how hard it was to let herself be held. Not trusting that anyone would reliably be there for her, she had based her life on being independent, as a way of compensating for the lack of holding in her childhood. So to shift gears and let herself feel held was scary. It threatened her stance as a self-made woman and made her feel acutely vulnerable. As the session ended I encouraged her to keep exploring her wish to feel held in the week between sessions.

Before the next session, Sarah had a minor car accident and wound up calling Eric for support and help. He was delighted to take care of her for the weekend, and this felt comforting to her. Yet though she felt comforted in Eric's arms, she also realized that this wasn't nearly as powerful as the presence of holding she had felt in my office the previous week.

Later that week Sarah attended a funeral for the father of her friend Jill, and she held Jill as she cried during the service. Later, when Jill thanked Sarah for comforting her, Sarah had a strange sense of "Don't thank me; I wasn't doing anything." Yes, she had embraced Jill in a caring way that felt warm and sweet. Yet at one point in the process she had felt a shift in Jill's body: Something had let go, and then Jill relaxed and landed on a ground of support in the midst of her grief, just as Sarah herself had done in my office the previous week. These two incidents helped Sarah start to develop a new and profound insight: that another person cannot actually provide the ultimate holding we most need.

During the next session Sarah started to connect the dots and realize that the shift that had happened in Jill's body was similar to something she had often experienced in my office. For years Sarah had remarked on how different she felt in my office than in her life outside. In her life, she ran around putting out fires, taking care of people, struggling with to-do lists, and generally feeling harried and stressed. Here in the office she was able to settle down, relax, consciously experience her feelings, connect with herself, and enter into a deeper quality of presence, which was both calming and strengthening. Why, she would often ask, can't I feel like this on my own at home?

All these years Sarah had experienced our work as a hold-ing environment that helped her be herself more fully. In one sense it's true, I was holding her experience, just as she had held her friend at the funeral. I provided an environment of attentive listening and presence that welcomed her ex-perience in an attuned, accepting way. The warm human connectedness between us had been deeply healing for her and had allowed her to learn new ways of relating to herself and others. Indeed, this kind of holding environment is the bedrock of therapeutic healing.

Yet in a deeper sense, my holding presence allowed her to relax and open into her own ground. And when she did this, she found a larger holding that was already naturally there. Through experiencing this holding, she was able to discover the support of a larger warmth and presence that held her whole existence.

Now I could say something she was finally ready to hear: "You feel held when you're here in this office, but in truth I'm not really doing the holding, any more than you were holding Jill's grief at the funeral, or than Eric was holding your pain over the weekend. You were lovingly present with Jill's grief, but you couldn't hold her grief, because only she was having her experience. The same thing is happening here. Only you are having your feelings, so I can't literally hold them. But my attunement to what you are feeling helps you find the strength to meet and open to what you're going through. When you're open like that, you're finally there for yourself. And then you discover what is always holding you."

"How can I hold myself at home like that?" Sarah asked.

"*You* can't hold yourself. It's not the *I* that is doing the holding, just as I as a therapist can never really hold your ex-perience. When I am here for you, it helps *you* be here for you.

And when you are here for you—*that* is what gives you the experience of feeling held."

Just as the vast expanse of sunlit space is always nurturing and cradling the earth, so too the warmth and openness of our larger being, our love-nature, is always holding and surrounding us, whether we know it or not. The only thing that separates us from this larger presence is our tendency to turn away from our experience or shroud ourselves in the clouds of defensiveness.

Different spiritual traditions describe this true ground in different ways. Christians, Jews, and Muslims say that God is holding us—that He has the whole world in His hands. Other traditions say the Divine Mother always holds us in Her arms. Buddhists say we live within the expanse of open, compassionate awareness—the Buddha-nature within each of us. (The Buddhist term for the fundamental law of existence— *Dharma*—literally means "that which holds.") Whatever the religious language, this holding is regarded as vast and spacious, as well as benevolent and kind.

The lack of holding in Sarah's childhood had caused her to contract and try to hold herself up. This made it hard for her to recognize this larger holding. But with these realizations, that began to change. As she warmed up to being there for herself, she developed a new sense of life holding her in a benevolent way. And this brought new confidence and strength. She ended therapy not long afterward.

A year or so later, I ran into Sarah at a social event. I asked her how things were going, and she told me she was in a new relationship that seemed to be working. For a long time after ending with Eric, she had given up looking for a relationship, focusing instead on being there for herself. "That was a rich time for me. It was the first time I had ever been able to fully enjoy myself and my life without a man. I learned to appreciate each day, not for what I was accomplishing, but for the experience of being alive. It was like having an intimate relationship with myself, and with my own life. I saw how I had previously thrown away this treasure to go begging for love from others instead."

After six months, Sarah met a new man, but she didn't find him terribly interesting at first. She hadn't felt a great need to get involved because she had been enjoying her alone time so much. "We spent some time together, and it was friendly but no big deal."

But then things gradually started to develop between them. He had also suffered some big disillusions with women. So they both entered into relationship without a lot of expectations. "Things seemed simple, we each liked what we saw, and our appreciation of each other deepened over time. We were able to accept each other in a simple way I haven't known before."

Having come to know that she was held in life's embrace, Sarah no longer expected a man to be the bedrock of her existence. And this was allowing her to experience a warmth of connection that becomes possible when a relationship is no longer burdened by expectations for total fulfillment.

Sarah went on to admit that she had spent most of her life dreaming about perfect love while blaming the men in her life for not measuring up. But recently something had changed. Instead of resenting their failings, she could now see how each of these men, all the way back to her father, was wounded. And even though their wounding had kept their love from fully shining through, she recognized that each had loved her in his own way. "I'm learning to focus on the ways I *have* been loved instead of the ways I haven't been."

I felt moved by Sarah's words and the sense of freedom coming through them. And I was reminded of the last year of my mother's life, when I was finally able to let go of my grievances about how she couldn't see me, and appreciate instead all the ways she had loved me. I remembered how liberating it had been to free up my heart like that.

Sarah had spent her whole life trying to find someone who could fill the hole of love that her childhood had left her with. But no one had ever been able to measure up. Finally forced back on herself, she learned to be there for herself and discover that her life was held in love. And this had freed her to have a simpler kind of relationship with a man, not so encumbered by the old struggles and dramas.

In bringing our conversation to a close, Sarah left me with these words: "It's quite something. Now that I don't expect as much, personal intimacy with a man is sweeter than ever before. My new relationship is far from ideal, but I'd say it's good enough. Maybe that's what knowing I am loved has given me—the ability to be satisfied with a good-enough lover. Even though human love isn't perfect . . . I'm still willing to play."

Exercises

THE EXERCISES PRESENTED HERE (arranged according to the corresponding chapters of the book) have proven helpful to people in my workshops and trainings. Many of these exercises involve looking within and answering key questions. You can answer the questions either through journal writing or by simply contemplating them. I suggest that you spend a few moments at the beginning of each exercise settling down, taking a few deep breaths, and feeling yourself present in your body.

Introduction
RECOGNIZING YOUR GRIEVANCE

This exercise will help you identify a central grievance pattern that is operating in your life and in your relationships. Bringing this adversarial grievance pattern to consciousness is the first step in becoming free of it.

1. Think of some difficult, stressful, or painful situation in one of your current relationships—with a friend, lover, spouse, colleague, or family member.

2. When you think of this difficult situation, how do you feel in your body? How does it affect you?

3. When we feel conflict with other people, we often set ourselves in opposition to them. In what way are you seeing the other person as an adversary here? Notice how that oppositional stance affects your nervous system. (For example, do you feel anxious, tense, or heavy?)

4. Ask yourself if this is an old, familiar battle that you're fighting here, one that's been going on your whole life. What's familiar about it? What does it go back to in your past? What is your old grievance against "the other" that is coming up again in this situation? Phrase it in one sentence, in the present tense, starting with "You . . ." and imagine saying it to the other person. (For example, "you don't see me," "you don't treat me right," "you just want to take advantage of me.")

5. Once you have stated the grievance, notice how it is linked to an old, familiar sense of "you don't love (see, appreciate, know) me as I am."

6. What is it like to acknowledge this old grievance about not being loved, and to see how it still remains alive in you, affecting your interactions with others? It's important not to judge it. Instead, see how it feels just to bring it out in the open and recognize it.

Chapter 1
EXPLORING LOVE AS AN INNER EXPERIENCE

This exercise will help you explore the experience you are most wanting in a love relationship. Shifting your focus to your inner experience helps move the locus of power from "out there" to "in here," so that you are not totally dependent on an external relationship for what you most need inside.

In this exercise you will be repeatedly asking and answering key questions. This is best done in pairs, but if you don't have a partner to do it with, you can also ask yourself the questions and then pause and contemplate before answering them. Answer whatever first comes to mind without thinking too hard about your response.

1. Facing each other, one of you asks a question (listed below), and the other person looks within and then answers in a sentence or two. Then the questioner asks the question again and the responder answers again. There is no other dialogue during the exercise. This process continues for 5 to 10 minutes.

The repeating-question format is designed to help you inquire further into the issue at hand. Each time the question is asked, you can look more deeply within yourself. In this particular exercise there are two questions that are asked sequentially:

What kind of love do you most long for?
And what would that really give you?

The first question invites you to get in touch with how you most want to be loved. Give yourself full permission when answering this to say what you really want. The second question asks you to consider what having that would give you on the inside. In other words, what is the inner experience you most want from feeling loved? For example, the exercise might go something like this:

Questioner: What kind of love do you most long for?

Responder: I want to feel known and understood.

Questioner: And what would that really give you?

Responder: That would give me a sense of belonging.

Questioner: What kind of love do you most long for?

Responder: I want to know that someone wants me just as I am.

Questioner: And what would that really give you?

Responder: Then I could relax and feel more trusting.

2. At the end of 5 or 10 minutes, the questioner and the responder switch roles. At the conclusion of the exercise, you can talk together about how it feels to acknowledge the love you most long for and what that would give you. If you do this exercise alone, take some time to feel the effect of recognizing these things.

To Feel Loved Is to *Be* Love

This exercise will help you explore how being loved allows the window of the heart to open, so that you can experience love as something within you, rather than something that someone hands over to you.

1. Think of someone in your life who loves you—a lover, spouse, friend, or family member. Let yourself feel this person's love and caring for you.
2. Notice how you associate this good feeling with the other person, and how you tend to see the other as the cause or source of it.
3. Now let go of thinking about the other person and pay attention to what happens in your body when you feel loved. Pay particular attention to the heart center, the area at the center of your chest. See if you can recognize the

warmth or fullness in your heart *as your own experience*, as something that arises from within you, as something that is yours.

4. How does it feel to recognize that?

Chapter 2
RECOGNIZING YOUR INVESTMENT IN GRIEVANCE

This exercise allows you to explore and name the hidden payoff in holding on to your grievance against others. You can do the repeating-question part of this exercise with someone else or by yourself.

1. Come back to the grievance you articulated in the first exercise, entitled "What's your grievance?"
2. Acknowledge any way in which it feels good to hold on to this grievance. See if you can recognize and admit the satisfaction you take in making the other person wrong.
3. What does making the other wrong give you on the inside? What does it do for you? If you could prove to this person and have this person accept that he or she is wrong, what would you get from that?
4. This next step involves a repeating question:
   What's good about holding on to this grievance?
   (One person asks this question and the other person looks within and then answers in a sentence or two. Then the questioner asks again and the responder answers again. There is no other dialogue during the exercise. This process continues for 5 to 10 minutes. Then the questioner and responder change roles.)
5. Each time you respond to this question, explore and describe the benefit you derive from holding on to your

grievance. It's important not to judge yourself in any way but just to let yourself see what's true in a neutral, inquisitive way.

THE BAD OTHER

This exercise will help you see how bad-other projections operate in your relationships.

1. Think of a recent conflict with your partner, or anyone else, where you felt badly treated, misunderstood, or hurt in some way.
2. Acknowledge how that sense of mistreatment feels to you, particularly any anger or frustration associated with it.
3. When feeling your anger or frustration, how does the other person look to you? What bad-other picture comes up? (For instance, you might see the other as indifferent, hostile, invasive, rejecting, abandoning, or controlling.)
4. Now ask yourself: How is this bad-other picture familiar to you, going back all your life? What does it remind you of from your childhood?
5. Recognizing this bad-other picture as something that you bring with you from your past, see if you can lift it off the person with whom you are relating in present time.
6. What is it like to see this person apart from the old bad-other picture?

Chapter 3
MELTING GRIEVANCE INTO GRIEF: MEETING YOURSELF IN THE PLACE OF UNLOVE

This is the process of unconditional presence applied to the pain of unlove, as described in chapter 3.

1. Think of some way you don't feel fully loved in a present relationship in your life—with a lover, friend, or family member.

2. How do you experience this sense of unlove in your body? Notice the specific quality of the bodily sensations (such as heavy, anxious, tight, nervous, cold, empty, numb, hot, thick, dull) and where in your body you feel them most strongly.

3. Acknowledge the feeling and the sensations that are there, directly contacting them with your awareness. If you feel tight or constricted, let your breath touch and permeate the sensation of tension.

4. Then see if you can let the feeling of unlove be there just as it is, without trying to fix it, change it, or judge it. Open up space around the sensations in your body, giving them plenty of room to be there just as they are. Experience the sensations being held in that soft, open space.

    What's it like to acknowledge and allow the sense of unlove and the sensations that go with it?

    If it feels bad to acknowledge and allow a feeling, this probably means you are rejecting or identifying with it rather than fully allowing it and giving it room to be there. The question here is not, "How does the place of unlove feel?" (yes, it may feel painful), but rather, "How does it affect you to contact that place and allow it room to be as it is?" If you feel stuck in or oppressed by the pain, place more attention and emphasis on the space of awareness surrounding the pain. As space, it is soft. The pain may still be there, but the act of allowing it to be there is not itself painful. Usually it feels more like a relief, though not always right at first.

    Also gently put aside any stories about yourself that

may come up as you meet the sense of unlove (such as "This means I'm unlovable," "It's bad to feel like this," "If I let myself feel this, I'll become depressed").

If strong resistance to the pain of unlove comes up and becomes an obstacle, it's best to shift your focus to the resistance itself. Resistance is understandable: It simply means not wanting to feel this pain. So you can acknowledge the resistance and give it room to be there as well. The pain and the resistance can each have their own space without having to cancel each other out. After making a separate space for the resistance to be there, you can then come back to the pain and continue working with it. Or if the resistance remains intense, then you can practice unconditional presence with it instead of with the original feeling.

Steps 1–4 may be enough to learn and practice for a while at first.

5. If you feel ready to go further, see if you can open yourself to the pain of unlove directly, letting down any barrier you may be maintaining against it. Can you open your heart to this pain, as a present, bodily felt experience? If so, see what that openness feels like.

6. A more advanced step: Having opened to the pain, now let your awareness enter right into the center of it. See if you can relax or let go into the sensations and become one with them. How does it affect you to be present right in the middle of the feeling that's there?

Summary: Acknowledging the feeling is like meeting it. Allowing it is letting the feeling be there as it is. Opening is like opening a door to it and facing it directly, without turning away or shielding yourself from it. And entering it is like walking through that door and taking up residence right in the center of the feeling. If you can work with the sense of unlove in this way, it will help you tolerate that feeling and realize that you are bigger than it, and therefore no longer have to live in fear of it.

OWNING YOUR ANGER OR HATRED

Be aware that you may not be ready for this exercise at this time. People often need to work with their grief and hurt for a long time before they are ready to deal with their buried anger or hatred. If this is true for you, it is important to respect that. In that case, work more with the previous exercise.

It's also important to distinguish between allowing yourself to feel anger or hatred and acting it out against others. This exercise is simply about helping you to let yourself have the feeling. It doesn't imply that you must express these feelings to anyone. (Communicating anger can be important at times, but doing that in a productive way is a dedicated practice that is beyond the scope of this book.)

1. Think of a grievance you have toward someone in your life (for example, your parents or a lover who has not treated you well).
2. Can you acknowledge your feelings of anger or hatred toward that person? Don't focus on this person's crimes but, rather, on the sensations of anger or hatred in your body. Acknowledge these sensations without becoming carried away by judgment or stories of blame, guilt, or shame. If those stories come up, gently put them aside and come back to the bodily feeling.
3. Give the anger or hatred plenty of space to be there. It's like a fire—if you keep the fire enclosed in a small space, it

becomes like a pressure cooker that wants to explode. You can take the pressure off by opening up space around the feeling and allowing the anger or hatred to expand into that space. The feeling can expand to fill the whole room, the whole neighborhood, or the whole world. Breathe deeply. What is it like to let it expand out into space instead of keeping it compressed in your body?

This might be enough to do at first. If you want to go further:

4. Let the hatred have a voice. As though you were holding a microphone up to the feeling, invite it to say what it hates. You could repeat the following statement several times until you have expressed everything that is there: "I hate it when . . ."

5. Notice how you feel once you have given the hatred a voice. Does any sense of clarity, strength, or power become available? If so, open to that and feel it in your body.

Chapter 4
DEVELOPING UNCONDITIONAL PRESENCE: LETTING
YOURSELF HAVE YOUR EXPERIENCE

This process is described more fully in chapters 3 and 4. In chapter 3 and the exercises for that chapter, it is presented as "meeting yourself in the place of unlove." Here it is presented in a broader way that can apply to any feeling. The four main steps are acknowledging, allowing, opening, and entering.

1. Choose some experience in your life to focus on that you're having difficulty with.

2. See if you are willing to turn toward this experience and explore how it affects you.

3. How does it feel in your body? Pay attention to the sensa-

tions and where in your body you feel them. *Acknowledge* what you're feeling, just as it is, meeting it directly, making contact with how it feels in your body. (This is like saying hello to it.) What is it like to contact and acknowledge this feeling?

4. Having acknowledged the presence of these sensations in your body, see if you can then *allow* them to be there, giving them plenty of space to be just as they are. Hold the feeling in the space of awareness without:

   - reacting to it,
   - judging it,
   - trying to change or fix it,
   - getting caught in it,
   - identifying with it,
   - making it mean something about you, or
   - hardening against it.

   Let yourself soften around it as the sky holds a cloud, without resistance, simply letting it be, or like a mother holding a baby, with gentleness and caring.

   What is that like? How does it feel to allow it and give it space to be there, just as it is?

   That might be enough to do for right now. If you want to go further:

5. See if you can *open* yourself, open your heart, to this feeling, letting down any barrier between you and it. Open directly to the sensations that are happening in your body. Pay attention to the feeling of the openness. What is that like?

6. Having opened to the sensations in your body, let your awareness relax and *enter* directly into the center of them and be one with them. This is like taking up residence

there, coming alive in a place where you are usually shut down. What is it like to inhabit this feeling with awareness?

7. Does anything new become available (such as relief, peace, expansiveness, groundedness, strength) when you allow, open to, and inhabit the feeling? If so, acknowledge and open to this new feeling that has emerged through this practice, paying attention to how it is in your body. This will help your body become accustomed to it, integrating the new experience.

Saying Yes to Yourself

This is a shorthand version of unconditional presence, which you can apply in the midst of your daily life situations.

Every day, at any time, you can simply notice what is happening in your experience, touching it lightly with your awareness: "Yes, this is here right now: I'm afraid . . . I am giving myself a hard time . . . I'm disconnected from myself," and so on.

Don't try to manipulate your experience or arrive at some better place. Rather, simply touch your experience, like putting your finger on a touch-screen computer. Contact the experience with your awareness and let it be as it is. If you start to judge the experience, you can touch that too: "Yes, I'm judging myself right now. Yes, I'm having a hard time accepting myself right now." Touch it and let it be. There's no need to make your experience right or wrong. It's just what is right now, neither good nor bad in itself.

A slight variation of this practice is to let yourself open to and be touched by what you're experiencing, rather than actively touching it. Let it touch you and then let it be. This may allow further softening toward what you're experiencing.

Kind Understanding for Yourself

This exercise can help you let go of grievances you hold against yourself.

1. Consider some way that you get down on yourself, give yourself a hard time, judge or hate yourself.
2. What's the grievance you have against yourself?
3. Notice how it feels to hold on to that grievance, how it affects your nervous system. (For example, does it make you anxious, contracted, subdued, or depressed?)
4. Consider how the problem you are judging has developed out of not feeling loved.
5. Recognizing that, see if you can hold what you're judging in kind understanding, as though you were a wise, all-knowing, all-compassionate parent, teacher, or friend.
6. What words of understanding would this wise one say to you?
7. How do those words affect you?
8. To conclude, see what it feels like to hold your judgment of yourself in an open space of nonjudgmental awareness.

Loving-Kindness

I am including two loving-kindness exercises here that involve saying certain phrases silently to yourself while in a contemplative mood. These phrases are not meant to be auto-suggestions or positive affirmations. The purpose is not to fabricate or crank up loving-kindness, but to let these phrases resonate within you and to explore the experience you have while repeating them.

Begin by sitting quietly and taking a few breaths. (If you meditate, you can do this practice as part of a meditation session.) Say a phrase silently a few times and then just let it resonate within you before going on to the next phrase. You can repeat the set of phrases as many times as you like.

LOVING-KINDNESS PART ONE. The first exercise is more psychologically oriented; it is directed toward the wounded place within yourself. This can be especially potent at times when you're feeling your wound, your vulnerability, or the pain of unlove. You can also speak each phrase directly to the wounded child within you, if that helps.

1. May I feel loved.
2. May I know that I am held in love.
3. May I know that love is my intrinsic nature.

LOVING-KINDNESS PART TWO. The second exercise is more spiritually oriented, because it involves encouraging yourself to live in the space of the open heart. On the inbreath, breathe into the heart center, in the center of your chest, and then say the phrase silently on the outbreath. Say each one a few times before moving on to the next. After saying each phrase a few times, take a few breaths in silence, letting yourself feel what it evokes. (These phrases are taken, with minor adaptation, from Ezra Bayda's excellent book *Being Zen: Bringing Meditation to Life*.)

1. May I dwell in the open heart.

    After saying this phrase, sense what is there. If you feel heart energy, openness, or warmth, let yourself experience that. If you feel nothing, let that be, and repeat the phrase again on the outbreath.
2. May I attend to whatever clouds the heart.

    After saying this, notice any obstacles to the open heart that may be present, such as impatience, fear, irritation, apathy, resentment, or judgment. See if you can simply extend the warmth of loving-kindness toward these mind-states, like letting the sun's rays touch the clouds in the sky. Don't judge or try to correct anything.

3. May I be awake in this moment just as it is.

   This is a more general encouragement to say yes to whatever you are experiencing. After speaking this phrase, simply be aware of whatever sensations, perceptions, feelings, or thoughts are present right now, letting them all be there just as they are.

4. May the heart in all beings be awakened.

   With this phrase, have a sense of extending loving-kindness to all beings. You are doing this by wishing that their heart be awakened, that they gain access to the open heart—which is the source of true peace and joy. You can start by thinking of someone close to you, wishing this for that person. Then you could extend that out to all beings, especially those who are suffering, lost, or disconnected from themselves. If you like, you can imagine specific populations on the planet who are suffering or acting out aggression.

5. May I dwell in the open heart.

   You can end the practice by repeating this first phrase again.

Chapter 5
IDENTIFYING OBSTACLES TO RECEIVING LOVE

This exercise involves a repeating question to help you see what obstacles you have to receiving love. As with the other repeating-question exercises, it is best done in pairs. If you don't have a partner to work with, you can ask yourself the questions, pause to contemplate them, then answer aloud or by writing in a journal.

1. One person asks: What's scary about opening to love and letting it all the way in? The other person looks within and then answers in a sentence or two. Then the questioner asks again, and the responder answers again. There is no other dialogue during the exercise. This process continues for 5 to 10 minutes.

2. The questioner and responder change roles.

3. Once you have identified your deep fears about letting love in, see if you can hold these fears in the space of loving-kindness. Be the space of awareness that holds them in warmth and openness.

OPENING TO YOUR LONGING FOR LOVE

This exercise helps you experience the energy of your longing as a way to open up your capacity to receive.

1. Notice some way in which you feel cut off from love right now.

2. How does this separation from love affect you in your body?

3. In this feeling of separation, notice if there is any longing to be more connected with love.

4. Now turn toward this inner longing and let yourself feel it directly.

5. Open to the energy of the longing as an experience in your body. Drop all focus on the outer object or on ideas about fulfilling the longing. Stay with the energy of your deep wish for love. Let that longing touch you.

6. What happens when you open to the longing? What's your experience?

Chapter 6
ABSOLUTE LOVE PRACTICE

This is a condensed version of the practice presented in chapter 6.

1. *Settle into your body.* Spend a few moments settling into your body and taking a few deep breaths.

2. *Acknowledge your separation from love.* Acknowledge some way in which you feel cut off or separate from love in your life. See how the lack of love feels in your body and feel that directly.

3. *Feel the energy of your longing.* In the place where you feel separate from love, notice your longing to feel more connected. Acknowledge your desire to be held in love, to be loved as you are.

   Open to the pure energy of this wish or longing without focusing on trying to get anything from anybody in particular. Feel the energy contained in the longing and let your attention rest in this bodily feeling. Sense the natural desire of the heart to abide in all-embracing, pure love.

4. *Open the heart and crown centers.* Feel the energy of your longing in your heart center, in the center of your chest. As the energy of the longing stirs, notice any way your heart seems to come alive or open. Let your crown center, at the top and back of your head, also become soft and receptive. Feel this receptive openness in both the heart and the crown centers.

5. *Let yourself receive.* Notice the desire to receive love that is contained in your longing. What that desire is essentially saying is, "I want to let you enter me." Let yourself acknowledge and feel that yes to receiving.

As you open to receiving, check and see: Is there any presence of love at hand right now? Don't think about it or look too hard. Rather, sense this very softly, very subtly: Is the presence of love available right now, is it anywhere at hand? Don't imagine or fabricate anything with your mind. Don't make it up. Simply experience what's there.

If there is some sense of warmth or love at hand, let it enter you, let your pores drink it in. Feel the cells of your body bathing in the presence of love.

Give yourself plenty of time to be with whatever you're experiencing.

6. *Let yourself melt and let love hold you.* Feeling the presence of love, let yourself relax and melt into it. Let yourself be held by love. Soften the boundaries of the body and feel what it's like to melt into this warmth.

Can you feel love as a gentle presence that holds you, allowing you to relax and let go? Instead of having to hold yourself up, let love be your ground.

MAY YOU BE HAPPY

This simple practice for extending loving-kindness to others is taken from the book *Tonglen* by Pema Chödrön, an American Buddhist nun. (This book contains many other valuable practices and discussions of loving-kindness and compassion as well.)

Here is the practice as Pema Chödrön describes it:

Walk down the street, perhaps for just one or two blocks, with the intention of staying as open as possible to whomever you meet. This is a training in being more emotionally honest with yourself and being more emotionally available to others. As you are walking . . . have the feeling that the area of your heart and chest is open. As you pass people, you might even feel a subtle connection between their heart and yours, as if you and they were linked by an invisible cord. You could think to yourself, "May you be happy," as you pass them. The main point is to feel a sense of interconnectedness with all the people you meet.

Pema advises noticing without judgment the thoughts and feelings that arise as you pass each person. Notice whatever you go through: fear, aversion, judging, shutting down, or opening up. Be kind and nonjudgmental toward yourself in this process as well.

This can be a good practice to do whenever you find yourself judging or blaming someone. Let that judgment be a reminder to say silently to that person, "May you be happy." This is a great act of compassion for yourself as well, as it immediately reduces inner stress.

Acknowledgments

I WOULD LIKE TO THANK my wife, Jennifer, as well as my editor, Eden Steinberg, for editing the manuscript and giving me helpful suggestions, and also for their enthusiastic support of the book. I also want to express appreciation for the students and clients I have worked with, whose struggle to find, honor, and open their hearts has been a source of inspiration and learning for me. Finally, I want to acknowledge Arnaud Desjardins for the chapter on absolute love in his book, *Toward the Fullness of Life,* which was one of several influences that originally sparked my engagement with the themes of this book.

Notes

Introduction

7 *These simple truths are also upheld by neuroscience research*   See, for example, Thomas Lewis, Fari Amini, and Richard Lannon, *A General Theory of Love* (New York: Random House, 2000).

8 *"Life is love and love is life"*   Nisargadatta Maharaj, *I Am That* (Durham, N.C.: Acorn Press, 1982, p. 75).

10 *the vital center in the belly*   I am using the term *vital center* here to refer to what the Japanese call *hara* and the Chinese call the lower *tan-tien*, which is located three or four fingerwidths below the navel, back toward the spine. All Asian systems of yoga regard this area as the body's center of gravity. Its cultivation is central to all martial arts disciplines, for someone who is not rooted in the vital center is easily knocked over.

   In a larger sense, the *vital center* could also refer to all three lower chakras, or energy centers in the body: the perineum, or sexual center; the point just below the navel; and the power center at the solar plexus. In this wider sense, the constricting of the vital center creates blockages in the areas of personal power, eros/sex, desire, grounding, emotional balance, and instinctual knowing.

13 *"We must love one another or die"*   From Auden's poem, "September 1, 1939."

13 *political settlements that lack genuine caring and respect for all parties eventually fall apart and lead to new conflicts*   The heavy-handed reparations required from Germany after World War I, for example, led to the even greater hatred and strife of World War II. The political unification of Yugoslavia did not resolve the old ethnic hatreds operating in Serbia and Kosovo that led to the Kosovo war. And the political settlements attempted thus far between Israel and Palestine have lacked the caring and respect that could end the bloodshed there.

13 *For example, Martin Luther King Jr.*   Doreen Rappaport, ed., *Martin's Big Words* (New York: Hyperion, 2001).

   Similarly, the Dalai Lama has argued that "Love and compassion have been omitted from too many spheres of social interaction for too long. Usually confined to family and home, their practice in public life is considered impractical, even naive. This is tragic." In *The Global Community and the Need for Universal Responsibility.* (Somerville, Mass.: Wisdom Publications, 1992).

14 *Then there is "grievance politics"*   The political division between the left wing and the right wing, and the intense antagonism accompanying it (especially in America), grow out of two opposite ways of responding to the love-wound from childhood. One way that children cope with their helplessness, pain, and powerlessness in families where they are not loved well is through a psychological defense called "identification with the aggressor." This involves identifying with the punitive parent (usually the father) who is in the position of strength: "If I can be like him, I will be safer." In this way the child finds a semblance of power in a powerless situation. This is the psychological strategy of those who wind up on the extreme right.

   Thus the right advocates for law and order, national security, tough measures, gun ownership, the privileged position of the wealthy power elite, and patriotism (from the Latin root, *pater,* father). Since this character structure is built on denying one's woundedness, right-wingers generally have little sympathy for the downtrodden, often demonizing them as "welfare cheats," losers, or misfits. For them, America and industrial civilization are the adult world, while those in third-world, underdeveloped countries are seen as irresponsible children who must be kept in line and told what to do. This attitude forms the basis for colonialism, empire building, and totalitarian tendencies that suppress popular dissent.

This need of people on the right to see themselves as strong and resolute, rather than helpless or weak explains why working people often vote for tough right-wing leaders who actually work against their economic interests. For it is more important to maintain the identification with the strong leader (parent) than to look out for their own interests (as children). This allows them to feel safe, through avoiding having to face their own woundedness and fear. Meanwhile, they have a horror of "bleeding-heart liberals" who sympathize with the wounded and oppressed. Voting for compassionate liberals, even though this might actually improve their economic security, would undermine the whole sense of identity their emotional security rests on.

Those on the left, on the other hand, usually identify instead with the victimized child, who is at the mercy of the unfair, insensitive, or oppressive parent. Because they acknowledge and feel the pain of their woundedness, they are attracted to an approach based on compassion and social justice. Thus the left advocates for workers' rights, social safety nets that take care of the poor and downtrodden, and a more fair and humane foreign policy. (My view is in accord with George Lakoff's model of the strict-parent right versus the nurturant-parent left, but emphasizes the psychological dimension of how these two poles arise out of different strategies for relating to the love-wound.)

However, a large number of people on the left are so identified with their victim identity that they cannot trust power or anyone in power. This accounts for the strange situation where progressives often shoot themselves in the foot, sabotaging any possibility of holding the reins of power—for example, by refusing to modify their idealistic principles in order to build a broad coalition that could rule, by acting out their pique with the established order in self-indulgent ways that turn the larger populace against them, or by voting for third-party candidates who have no chance of winning, thereby ensuring victory by the right. The rallying cry becomes, "We've been wronged and we aren't going to play with you."

Thus the left and the right represent opposite ways of dealing with one and the same wound: not feeling loved, cared for, and respected. And their mutual antagonism and lack of dialogue grow out of the vital threat they represent to one another. The right, representing the authoritarian, punitive parent, terrifies the left, which remains on guard against creeping fascism and police-state incursions on civil rights. The permissiveness of the left in turn terrifies the right, which remains on guard against erosion of rigid moral principles, lack of patriotism, and softness on crime—all of which threaten to undermine the strong-parent stance that provides their sense of security.

19 *"To love is to cast light"*   Ulrich Baer, ed., *The Poet's Guide to Life: The Wisdom of Rilke* (New York: The Modern Library, 2005).

Prologue

29 *And growing children are held within a family environment* At
the deepest level, human existence is held, supported, and
made possible by the fundamental way that reality works, the
basic principles known in the West as Divine Law and in the
East as the Way or the Dharma (which literally means "that
which holds"). In a culture like ours that no longer recognizes
or understands the natural, sacred order of things, it becomes
more difficult and rare for families to provide a balanced holding environment that nurtures sanity, confidence, and health.
Thus modern culture breeds people lacking an inner core of
well-being who find it difficult to love and be loved.

30 *When parents do provide enough of both contact and space* All too
often modern family life does not provide children with the
kind of contact or space they need for their development. Day
care, the use of television and computers as babysitting de-
vices, unstable marriages, busyness, and stress all work against
the all-important need for secure infant-mother bonding.

At the same time, the increasing tendency of parents to
keep children busy, occupied, and entertained works against
the child's need to spend time in unstructured states of being.
As Greenberg and Mitchell describe Winnicott's viewpoint on
this need for space:

> The mother's nondemanding presence makes the experi-
> ence of formlessness and comfortable solitude possible, and
> this capacity becomes a central feature in the development
> of a stable and personal self . . . . This makes it possible for
> the infant to experience . . . a state of 'going-on-being' out of
> which . . . spontaneous gestures emerge (Jay R. Greenberg
> and Stephen A. Mitchell, *Object Relations in Psychoanalytic
> Theory,* Harvard University Press, 1983, p. 193).

The interruption of "the experience of formlessness and comfortable solitude"—which Winnicott termed *impingement*—forces children to separate abruptly from the continuity of their "going-on-being." The child is then

> wrenched from his quiescent state and forced to respond . . . and to mold himself to what is provided for him. The major consequence of prolonged impingement is fragmentation of the infant's experience. Out of necessity he becomes prematurely and compulsively attuned to the claims of others . . . . He loses touch with his own spontaneous needs and gestures . . . [and develops] a false self on a compliant basis (*Ibid*).

Chapter 1: Perfect Love, Imperfect Relationships

35 *As Brother David Steindl-Rast describes this*   David Steindl-Rast, *Gratefulness: The Heart of Prayer* (Ramsey, N.J.: Paulist Press, 1984).

41 *As one Indian teacher, Swami Prajnanpad*   Swami Prajnanpad was an unusual and interesting Advaita Vedanta teacher who read Freud in the 1920s and developed his own version of psychotherapy for his students. He is not well known in the West outside of France. He had a small ashram in Bengal and died in 1974. The quotes from him in this book come from letters and transcripts of conversations he had with his French students. Although his work has not been available in English, Hohm Press (Prescott, Arizona) is preparing a book on his teachings by one of his main French students.

41 *"This is the exalted melancholy of our fate"*   Martin Buber, *I and Thou* (New York: Scribners, 1958, pp. 16–17).

46 *Yet this also gives rise to one of the most fundamental of all human illusions that the source of happiness and well-being lies outside us*

I am by no means suggesting that relative human love is dispensable or advocating that we should transcend our need for it. To the contrary, in other books I have argued that the challenges of human relationship provide important stepping-stones for personal and spiritual development. I have also argued against the notion, common in certain circles, of spiritual practice as a way to transcend involvement in the relational play of duality, of I and Thou. See John Welwood, "Double Vision: Duality and Nonduality in Human Experience," in *The Sacred Mirror*, John Prendergast, Peter Fenner, and Sheila Krystal, eds. (St. Paul, Minn.: Paragon House, 2003). The attempt to use spiritual ideas and practices to avoid dealing with emotional unfinished business—notably our woundedness around love—usually has disastrous consequences, especially in the West, frequently leading to psychological imbalance and destructive behavior. My term for this kind of dissociation and denial is *spiritual bypassing*.

Often we deal with our disconnection from love through one of two extremes: emotional denial— trying to rise above our wounding through worldly achievement or spiritual transcendence (a popular male choice)—or emotional fixation— becoming endlessly preoccupied with relationship as the source of all happiness (a popular female choice). In this book, I am proposing a middle way between these two extremes— through appreciating the relative significance of personal love, while also recognizing that it can never contribute to absolute ease and satisfaction. There can be no doubt that healthy relationships contribute to human happiness. Yet this happiness ultimately arises from our capacity to connect with what is most real and true within us—which a loving relationship can help put us in touch with.

54 *George Orwell once wrote* George Orwell, "Reflections on Ghandi," in *Shooting an Elephant* (New York: Harcourt, 1984).

54 *Bringing absolute love into human form* Bernard Phillips, an early participant in the East-West dialogue in the 1960s, once wrote that "every human being with whom we seek relatedness is a *koan,* that is to say, an impossibility." Koans are riddles that students of Zen Buddhism must solve as steps along their spiritual development. Yet these riddles cannot be solved with the conceptual mind. The only true answer comes from a larger intuitive knowing that lies beyond ordinary thought. Nonetheless, the Zen student cannot help trying to think up the answer. He or she brings these conceptual answers to the master again and again, while the master gruffly dismisses these stratagems. Eventually the student becomes so frustrated that his or her mind gives up. And then something more pure can come through the student, from beyond himself or herself.

So when Bernard Phillips says that every human being is an impossibility, like a koan, he is also suggesting that authentic love arises from an unfathomable place within us, where we are able to let go and let be, free from the mind's interference. He goes on to say:

> There is no formula for getting along with a human being. No technique will achieve relatedness. I am impossible to get along with; so is each one of you; all our friends are impossible; the members of our families are impossible. How then shall we get along with them? One way is to try to circumvent the difficulties which they pose by applying psychology. This may remove the immediate difficulty, but it will not forge a relationship. In this context we do well to be mindful of the ever-present possibility of gaining the whole world through technique, but losing our souls, that is, our relatedness to reality.

If you are seeking a real encounter, then you must confront the koan represented by the other person. The koan is an invitation to enter into reality.

54 *In his book, Works of Love*   Søren Kierkegaard, *Works of Love* (Princeton: Princeton University Press, 1995).

56 *For, as the great Sufi poet Rumi sings*   From Rumi's poem "Zero Circle," translated by Coleman Barks.

Chapter 2: The Mood of Grievance

60 *While love can exist free of hatred*   Research in neuropsychology showing a correlation between impaired maternal bonding and inappropriate aggressive behavior also supports this view. See Lewis, Amini, and Lannon, *A General Theory of Love,* pp. 208–9.

Chapter 3: Letting Grievance Go

92 *Since it is easy to remember only the times when we think our mother harmed us*   This contemplation is condensed from a much longer version that appears in Kelsang Gyatso, *Joyful Path of Good Fortune* (Cumbria, England: Tharpa Publications, 2000, pp. 403–6).

Chapter 4: From Self-Hatred to Self-Love

98 *This notion of basic goodness*   I have taken the term *basic goodness* from the teachings of the Tibetan master Chögyam Trungpa Rinpoche. This was his translation of a Tibetan term that refers to the native purity and dignity of our being as well as the intrinsic wonder and delight of reality when seen clearly. See Chögyam Trungpa, *Shambhala: The Sacred Path of the Warrior* (Boston: Shambhala Publications, 1983).

103 *If Stalin, Hitler, or Osama bin Laden*   In her books *For Your Own Good* and *Paths of Life*, Alice Miller has researched the role of childhood lovelessness and wounding in the lives and development of vicious tyrants. Some relevant quotes from a lecture of hers ("The Childhood Trauma," delivered in New York City, 1998):

> I can certainly aver that I have never come across perse-
> cutors who weren't themselves victims in their childhood,
> though most of them don't know it because their feelings
> are repressed. The less these criminals know about them-
> selves, the more dangerous they are to society. So I think it
> is crucial to grasp the difference between the statement,
> "every victim becomes a persecutor," which is wrong, and
> the statement, "every persecutor was a victim in his child-
> hood," which I consider true.
>
> For Alois Hitler [Hitler's father] the suspicion that he
> might be of Jewish descent [it is likely that Hitler's grand-
> mother was impregnated by a Jewish employer] was insuf-
> ferable in the context of the anti-Jewish environment in
> which he was raised. . . . The only thing he could do with
> impunity was to take out this rage on his son Adolf. Ac-
> cording to the reports of his daughter . . . Alois beat his son
> mercilessly every day. In an attempt to exorcise his child-
> hood fears, his son nurtured the manic delusion that it was
> up to him to free not only himself of Jewish blood but also
> all Germany and later the whole world . . .
>
> Mao had been regularly whipped by his father and later
> sent 30 million people to their deaths, but he hardly ever ad-
> mitted the full extent of the rage he must have felt for his
> own father, a very severe teacher who had tried through
> beatings to "make a man" out of his son. Stalin caused mil-

lions to suffer and die because even at the height of his power his actions were determined by unconscious, infantile fear of powerlessness. Apparently his father, a poor cobbler from Georgia, attempted to drown his frustration with liquor and whipped his son almost every day. His mother displayed psychotic traits, was completely incapable of defending her son and was usually away from home. . . . Stalin idealized his parents right up to the end of his life and was constantly haunted by the fear of dangers, dangers that had long since ceased to exist but were still present in his deranged mind. His fear didn't even stop after he had been loved and admired by millions. ("The Childhood Trauma," New York, 1998)

Here we can see the mood of unlove at work.

111 *As the German spiritual teacher Rudi* Rudrananda, *Entering Infinity* (Portland, Ore.: Rudra Press, 1994, p. 23).

117 *In Buber's words* Martin Buber, *The Way of Man according to the Teaching of Hasidism* (Seacacus, N.J.: 1950, pp. 16–17).

Chapter 5: Holy Longing

127 *plainly wanting or needing something* Desire and need are close cousins. Need is a raw and more intense form of desire.

132 *In the words of the Indian teacher Nisargadatta* Nisargadatta Maharaj, *I Am That.*

133 *Our longing for more arises from what is infinite within us* Kierkegaard called this "infinite passion," or "passion for the infinite."

134 *The Indian teacher Sri Poonja* David Godman, ed., *Papaji* (Boulder, Colo.: Avadhuta Foundation, 1993, p. 72).

136 *Rumi calls this the "secret cup"* From Rumi's poem "Love Dogs," translated by Coleman Barks.

149 *This whole question of needing other people is a confusing and tricky one*   Some spiritual teachers say that emotional needs are an illusion—because everything we truly need for well-being and balance is contained within us, in our deepest essence. Most psychotherapists, on the other hand, would say that we can't help needing people, and that trying to transcend need is a form of denial or repression that diminishes our vitality and humanness.

    Both of these views contain a kernel of truth. Each of us is more or less dependent on others, according to our degree of maturity and inner development. At one end of the developmental continuum, the infant is dependent on others for everything. At the other end of the continuum are enlightened sages, who have become totally free of emotional dependency on others because they have discovered how to live at one with the source of all. Between these two ends of the developmental spectrum, most of us continue to have some emotional dependency and need for human warmth and connectedness, although the extent of this can evolve over the course of a lifetime. Thus the operative principle seems to be: "You need people until you don't."

150 *Just because we are fashioned out of absolute love, this does not mean that we can embody it*   Humanity discovered the reality of enlightenment and spiritual awakening thousands of years ago. This was an amazing discovery. Nonetheless, all the great attainments in the area of spiritual realization, wonderful as they are, have hardly begun to transform the overall quality of human relationships on this planet, which are still driven by the darkest motivations and emotions.

The hard truth is that spiritual awakenings often do not heal our deep wounding in the area of love, or translate readily into skillful communication or interpersonal attunement. Thus many spiritual adepts—teachers and students alike—either leave intimate relationships behind altogether or wind up having the same relational difficulties and problems that everyone else has.

Swami Prajnanpad recognized the discrepancy between people's spiritual practice and their ability to embody it in their relationships, often telling students who wanted to study with him to "bring a certificate from your wife." He saw marriage as a particularly powerful litmus test of one's development, because in it one is "fully exposed. . . . All one's peculiarities, all of one's so-called weaknesses are there in their naked form. This is why it is the testing ground." In solitary spiritual practice, the spiritual aspirant "may accomplish perfection and feel: 'Oh! I am at ease, oh, I can feel oneness.'" But in marriage, "everything gets confounded." Yogis discover that their so-called realization "was only on the superficial level. It had not percolated deep within. It simply appeared to have gone deep. Unless you are tested on the ground where you are fully exposed, all those outward achievements are false."

Thus it seems that complete human development entails two main kinds of ripening: *awakening,* which involves discovering and realizing one's true, absolute, essential nature, and *individuation,* which involves becoming a true person, someone who is capable of genuine contact, personal transparency, and intimacy with others. Since opening to absolute love allows us to recognize our essential nature *as* love, it is part of the path of awakening. Working on developing conscious relationships belongs to the path of individuation, for it is the means for evolving into a true person—someone who can embody love in an intimate, personal way.

157 *For as the Indian teacher Sri Poonja points out*   H. W. L. Poonja, *The Truth Is* (San Anselmo, Calif.: VidyaSagar Publications, 1995, p. 287).

159 *"You must fall in love with the one inside your heart"*   Ibid., p. 293.

About the Author

JOHN WELWOOD, PH.D., is a clinical psychologist, psychotherapist, teacher, and author. His innovative work integrates Eastern contemplative teachings with Western therapeutic understanding and practice. He leads popular workshops on conscious relationship and psychospiritual work throughout the world.

For more information, please visit his website at *www.johnwelwood.com*. If you would like to be on his mailing list, please send your e-mail and postal address to:

John Welwood
P.O. Box 2173
Mill Valley, CA 94942
(415) 381-6077

Books and Audio by John Welwood

Books

Awakening the Heart: East/West Approaches to Psychotherapy and the Healing Relationship

Can a meditative practice assist and promote the healing relationship between psychotherapist and patient? The notable contributors to this practical book draw on a wide range of Eastern and Western disciplines—psychoanalysis, Gestalt, Aikido, and various Christian, Hindu, and Buddhist contemplative traditions—to show that it can. Jacob Needleman, Erich Fromm, Robin Skynner, Ram Dass, Karl Sperber, Roger Walsh, Chögyam Trungpa, and Thomas Hora are among the contributors.

Challenge of the Heart: Love, Sex, and Intimacy in Changing Times

This powerful collection of essays by such notables as D. H. Lawrence, Robert Bly, Anne Morrow Lindbergh, and Rainer Maria Rilke focuses on the challenges of love between men and women, addressing the questions and difficulties arising for people in relationships today. Carefully selected, threaded together by John Welwood's insightful commentary, the essays presented here approach the challenge of intimacy with bravery and gentleness, inspiring the reader toward becoming a "warrior of the heart."

Ordinary Magic: Everyday Life as Spiritual Path

Spiritual practice and meditation are often thought of as being the province of priests, monks, and nuns—those few individuals who have returned from the preoccupations of day-to-day life. This inspiring book, composed of thirty-five essays written by well-known spiritual teachers, therapists, and creative artists, reveals how the simple practice of mindfulness can be a magical and transformative part of anyone's daily life.

Perfect Love, Imperfect Relationships: Healing the Wound of the Heart

This book takes the reader on a powerful journey of healing and transformation that involves learning to embrace our humanness and appreciate the imperfections of our relationships as trail-markers along the path to great love. It sets forth a process for releasing deep-seated grievances we hold against others for not loving us better and against ourselves for not being better loved. And it shows how our longing to be loved can magnetize the great love that will free us from looking to others to find ourselves.

Toward a Psychology of Awakening: Buddhism, Psychotherapy, and the Path of Personal and Spiritual Transformation

How can we connect the spiritual realizations of Buddhism with the psychological insights of the West? In *Toward a Psychology of Awakening* John Welwood addresses this question with comprehensiveness and depth. Along the way he shows how meditative awareness can help us develop more dynamic and vital relationships and how psychotherapy can help us embody spiritual realization more fully in everyday life.

Audio

Perfect Love, Imperfect Relationships: A Workshop on Healing the Wound of the Heart

In this audio program based on the book *Perfect Love, Imper-*

fect Relationships, John Welwood offers fresh and penetrating insight into our relationship problems. With understanding and encouragement, he explains that most of us carry an un-addressed emotional wound—a deep-seated, unconscious belief that we are not worthy of love. This belief causes us to close ourselves off from others and prevents us from experiencing the unconditional love we long for. In this transformative workshop, Welwood shows us how to acknowledge, examine, and heal this core emotional wound so we can receive love in a way that we never have before. 4 CDs, 4 1/2 hours.